FRISCO

In Color

High Noon of Frisco's first generation of diesel operation: three black GP-7's; a neatly renovated steam-era roundhouse now adapted to diesel maintenance; jointed rail; a yard full of on-line origin mixed traffic. It is August 15, 1961 in Ft. Smith, Arkansas.

(Louis A. Marre)

LOUIS A. MARRE - GREGORY J. SOMMERS

Acknowledgements

The Authors gratefully acknowledge material and technical assistance provided to them over the
course of many years by Frisco people, some now deceased: Robert Rorie, Joseph Sauerburger,
Thomas Temple, Frank Trau, Guler Worden and Sid Zeilman. For this specific book project, we have
benefitted from the cooperation not only of those individuals named in photo credits, but also in special ways to Joe G. Collias, P. Allen Copeland, Charles Dischinger, Glen P. Koshiol, Gordon E. Lloyd,
Gordon Lloyd, Jr., Arthur H. Peterson, David Sweetland and the Publisher, Robert J. Yanosey.

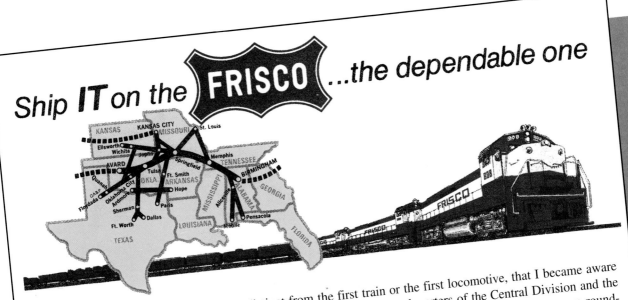

Ship **IT** on the **FRISCO** ...the dependable one

The Frisco was the first railroad, as distinct from the first train or the first locomotive, that I became aware of in any meaningful way. I was born in Ft. Smith, Arkansas, the headquarters of the Central Division and the location of a modest diesel shop, in which my maternal Grandfather had worked when it was a steam round-house. As I grew up, I studied the railroad with increasing sophistication, beginning by attempting photographs of locomotives and trains and then later by scrounging diagram books, assignment sheets, mileage reports and other sorts of locomotive documents from the roundhouse foreman and other employees. I gradually came to know the Company as I would the members of an extended family, "characters" and all.

In time, I moved away and "learned" other railroads; but the Frisco was always the standard by which others were measured, even the mighty New York Central, which had more passenger trains. But they never had quite the impact on my imagination as that made by my vision of the TEXAS SPECIAL roaring past the Webster Groves suburban depot in St. Louis, named scarlet E-8's up front and a red and silver train following, glittering in fading light. The Pennsylvania had more engines, but none quite measured up to a Ft. Smith VO-1000 in immaculate black and yellow, nearly purring. No! The Frisco was the standard railway of the world.

While I was elsewhere, the Frisco faded into another railroad. I had kept up with the roster and photographed on line whenever I could, but intervals between visits grew longer and longer until, at the end of 1980, not only could I not go home again, but even if I could, "my" railroad was no longer there.

Fortunately, the co-author of this book was there when I could not be. Greg was born in Chicago, and there-fore lacked the inestimable advantage of living on the Frisco. However, he made up for that handicap by devot-ing every available day to Frisco photography from 1973 until the end of the line in 1980. After that melancholy closure, it was inevitable that two such souls - so discerning, so enlightened, so appreciative of the finer things - should meet. We have, in the fifteen years since, tried to compensate for our lack of shared Frisco experiences. We now shamelessly embellish all our anecdotes, which get longer with each telling. We exaggerate every dif-ficulty which had to be overcome to get the shots. It is fortunate that we have photographs, or the truth would be very hard to find.

More than usual, this book is a monument to our notion of the ideal railroad, arrived at by separate paths but agreeing perfectly on the conclusion. It was a splendid operation, extremely well-run and carefully maintained. Almost without fear of contradiction, we assert that it had the greatest "atmosphere" of any railroad in its time. At least within these covers, it will remain forever. Since we cannot go home again, we have tried to achieve the next best thing: though the Frisco is not "there" anymore, it is here. LAM.

Louis A. Marre
Dayton, Ohio
March 5, 1995

Gregory J. Sommers
Chicago, Illinois
April 11, 1995

FRISCO

FRISCO DIESEL SUMMARY 1941-1980

Road Numbers	Builder and Model	Date Built	Notes
1 - 2	Davenport 44-ton	2/42	
3	Whitcomb 44-ton	4/43	
4 - 8	GE 44-ton	9/43 - 1/44	
10	EMD SW-1	9/41	Acquired 10/79
11	GE 45-ton	8/41	Acquired 1948
12	GE 70-ton	9/50	Acquired 8/64
60 - 61	Baldwin VO-660	5/41	Acquired 4/42
101-111	ALCO RS-1	11/44 - 8/46	Acquired 1948
100 - 124	EMD GP15-1	8/77	
200 - 237	Baldwin VO-1000	11/41 - 6/46	See repowering table
238 - 241	Bald. DS4-4-1000	12/48	
250 - 265	EMD NW-2	4/48 - 6/49	
270 - 281, 286	F-M H10-44	3/48 - 7/49	286 acquired 6/69
282 - 285	F-M H12-44	6/51	
290 - 297	Alco S-2	5/46 - 2/50	295-297 acq. 1/64
298	Alco S-4	7/52	Acquired 1/64
296 - 299	EMD SD38-2	6/79	
300 - 304	EMD SW-7	12/50	
305 - 314	EMD SW-9	1/52	
315 - 360	EMD SW1500	10/68 - 1/73	
361 - 365	EMD MP15DC	3/75	
400 - 478	EMD GP38-2	6/73 - 12/76	
500 - 549			
555-632	EMD GP-7	2/50 - 2/52	
550 - 554	Alco RS-2	10/49	See repowering table
633 - 662	EMD GP38-AC	2/71 - 4/71	
663 - 699	EMD GP38-2	3/72 - 11/72	
700-732	EMD GP35	3/64-12/65	
750 - 774	EMD GP40-2	4/79 - 6/79	
800 - 831	GE U25B	1/61 - 2/66	
832 - 862	GE U30B	10/68 - 3/75	
863 - 870	GE B30-7	12/77	
900 - 948	EMD SD45	2/67 - 12/69	
950 - 957	EMD SD40-2	7/78	
2000 - 2005	EMD E-7A	3/47	See name table
2006 - 2022	EMD E-8A	2/50 - 7/50	See name table
5000 - 5017	EMD F-3A	1/48 - 6/48	See renumbering table
5018 - 5039	EMD F-7A	3/49 - 5/50	See renumbering table
5040 - 5051	EMD FP-7	12/50 - 2/51	See renumbering table
5100 - 5117	EMD F-3B	1/48 - 6/48	See renumbering table
5118 - 5139	EMD F-7B	3/49 - 7/53	See renumbering table
5140 - 5152	EMD F-9B	1/54 - 4/57	See renumbering table
5200 - 5231	Alco FA-1	6/48 - 4/49	See repowering table and renumbering table
5300 - 5315	Alco FB-1	6/48 - 4/49	See repowering table and renumbering table

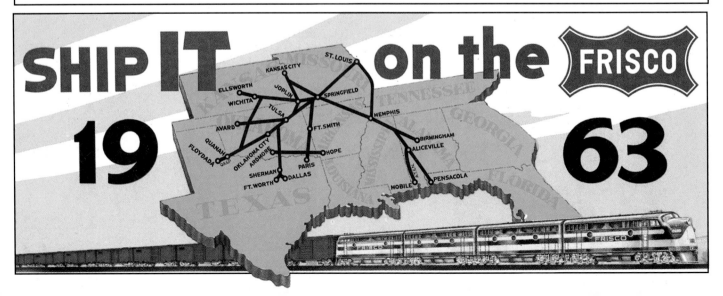

RENUMBERING TABLE

The Frisco never undertook a system-wide renumbering. The two VO-660's delivered in 1942 as SL-SF 600-601 were renumbered to 60-61 in 1950 to make room for additional GP-7's. After that the only renumbering of existing units (units acquired secondhand not included) took place in 1968 when the roster had to be cleared of four-digit numbers for simplification. Those units renumbered in 1968 are listed below.

Old Number	New Number	Model		Old Number	New Number	Model		Old Number	New Number	Model
5002	62	F-3A		5041	41	FP-7		5133	133	F-7B
5005	75	F-3A (rebuilt to F9M 2/54)		5042	42	FP-7		5134	134	F-7B
5006	66	F-3A		5043	43	FP-7		5135	135	F-7B
5007	77	F-3A (rebuilt to F9M 2/54)		5045	45	FP-7		5136	136	F-7B
5012	64	F-3A		5047	47	FP-7		5137	137	F-7B
5018	18	F-7A		5048	48	FP-7		5138	138	F-7B
5019	19	F-7A		5049	49	FP-7		5139	139	F-7B
5021	21	F-7A		5050	50	FP-7		5140	140	F-9B
5022	22	F-7A		5051	51	FP-7		5141	141	F-9B
5023	23	F-7A		5100	160	F-3B		5142	142	F-9B
5024	24	F-7A		5101	161	F-3B		5143	143	F-9B
5025	25	F-7A		5104	164	F-3B		5144	144	F-9B
5028	28	F-7A		5105	165	F-3B		5145	145	F-9B
5029	29	F-7A		5117	167	F-3B		5146	146	F-9B
5030	30	F-7A		5118	118	F-7B		5147	147	F-9B
5031	31	F-7A		5119	119	F-7B		5148	148	F-9B
5032	32	F-7A		5121	121	F-7B		5149	149	F-9B
5033	33	F-7A		5122	122	F-7B		5150	150	F-9B
5034	34	F-7A		5125	125	F-7B		5151	151	F-9B
5035	35	F-7A		5127	127	F-7B		5152	152	F-9B
5036	36	F-7A		5128	128	F-7B		5301	191	FB-1 (EMD repowered)
5037	37	F-7A		5129	129	F-7B		5303	193	FB-1 (EMD)
5038	38	F-7A		5130	130	F-7B		5307	197	FB-1 (EMD)
5039	39	F-7A		5131	131	F-7B		5309	199	FB-1 (EMD)
5040	40	FP-7		5132	132	F-7B		5310	190	FB-1 (EMD)

E-7 / E-8 NAME TABLE

Frisco E-7A and E-8A passenger units were named for famous horses. The names were applied in 1950. Units repainted from 1965 to the disposition of all passenger units did not retain their names.

2000	*Fair Play*		2008	*Messenger*		2016	*Citation*
2001	*Ranger*		2009	*Jet Pilot*		2017	*Pensive*
2002	*Comanche*		2010	*Count Fleet*		2018	*Ponder*
2003	*Steel Dust*		2011	*Gallant Fox*		2019	*Cavalcade*
2004	*Dan Patch*		2012	*Flying Ebony*		2020	*Big Red*
2005	*Winchester*		2013	*Sea Biscuit*		2021	*Gallahadion*
2006	*Traveller*		2014	*Truxton*		2022	*Middleground*; renamed
2007	*Whirlaway*		2015	*Twenty Grand*			*Champion*, 1952

FRISCO LOCOMOTIVES TRANSFERRED TO BURLINGTON NORTHERN OWNERSHIP NOVEMBER 1980

Frisco Number	Model	BN Number		Frisco Number	Model	BN Number
10	SW-1	70		675-699	GP38-2	2345-2369
100-124	GP15-1	1375-1399		700-722	GP35	2550-2572
250-265	NW-2	410-425		724-732	GP35	2574-2582
296-299	SD38-2	6260-6263		750-774	GP40-2	3040-3064
300-304	SW-7	75-79		808-831	U25B	5210-5233
305-314	SW-9	260-269		832-855	U30B	5770-5793
315-360	SW1500	20-65		857-862	U30B	5794-5799
361-365	MP15	1000-1004		863-870	B30-7	5485-5492
400-478	GP38-2	2255-2333		900-908	SD45	6650-6658
633-650	GP38AC	2110-2127		910-925	SD45	6659-6674
652-662	GP38AC	2128-2138		927-948	SD45	6675-6696
663-673	GP38-2	2334-2344		950-957	SD40-2	6840-6847

REPOWERING TABLE

The following locomotives were repowered with EMD prime movers on the dates shown. All repowering work was done by EMD at La Grange, IL.

Locomotives	Model	Dates
200-206; 210, 215	VO-1000	3/57 - 8/59
550-554	RS-2	11/59 - 10/60
5200-5209; 5211-5213; 5215-5219	FA-1	3/55-1/57
5300-5311	FB-1	4/55 - 2/57

FRISCO *In Color*

Though this present volume is concerned primarily with Frisco's diesel locomotives, and thus begins on November 23, 1941 with the purchase of a Baldwin VO-1000, those locomotives joined a business whose roots extend back to 1849. The history of that business deserves a brief survey at this point.

What we refer to as "the Frisco" began as a neglected stepchild of St. Louis's grand attempt to construct a "Pacific Railroad" and thus maintain its status as a preeminent trade center. A Pacific Railroad was chartered by a group of merchant-investors in 1849, and actual construction of a line of railroad toward the West began in 1852. While that construction was still going on in the general direction of Kansas City, a southwesterly branch was undertaken, diverging from the "main line" at Franklin (now Pacific) Missouri, in 1858. This branch line is the direct ancestor of the Frisco.

After the interruption to development caused by the Civil War, the branch became for a time the grandiosely-titled "Atlantic & Pacific RR Co." Under that name, the road passed Springfield, MO (in April of 1870) and reached Indian Territory in 1872. After some financial reorganization, the A&P became the "St. Louis & San Francisco Ry. Co." in 1876. What would be the Central Division of the Frisco was built southward from Monett, MO from 1876, aiming for Dallas but stopping at Paris, TX in 1886 and reaching Dallas by an agreement with Santa Fe. During these turbulent years of expansion, the StL&SF was at various times in the camps of the Missouri Pacific (its former parent), the Santa Fe, and the Southern Pacific. When the dust settled in 1896, the surviving entity was the "St. Louis & San Francisco RR Co." When Santa Fe control passed, so did the route to San Francisco - which the Frisco never reached on its own. For a short time in the 1880's, however, the Frisco/Santa Fe had advertised and run a through passenger service from St. Louis to San Francisco (see map).

Meanwhile, another series of companies had built a line of road from Kansas City to the bank of the Mississippi opposite Memphis. This line crossed the Frisco in Springfield, which by that time had become the center of SL&SF motive power maintenance as well as a *de facto* operating hub. Upon completion of its crown jewel, the first bridge across the mighty Mississippi at Memphis, the Kansas City, Fort Scott & Memphis Ry. (named KCFS&M for legal purposes, though constructed under the name of the Kansas City, Memphis & Birmingham) was promptly acquired by the SL&SF. By virtue of this timely acquisition, the Frisco effectively doubled in size, and greatly expanded its service territory and traffic potential.

Springfield, in the cross of the "X" formed by the merged companies, took on added importance in Frisco affairs.

From 1896 to 1916, the SL&SF fell prey to a syndicate of speculators, and for a time was controlled by the Rock Island. It also briefly exercised control over the Chicago & Eastern Illinois, and a collection of small lines between New Orleans and Brownsville loosely called the "Gulf Coast Lines." This paper empire collapsed in 1916. The C&EI regained its independence, the Gulf Coast Lines eventually became Missouri Pacific properties, and the reorganised survivor adopted a hyphen in place of an ampersand and became the St. Louis - San Francisco Ry. As the "Frisco" it remained until 1980, when it was merged into the Burlington Northern. The SL-SF was in receivership from September 26, 1933 to December 31, 1946, but did not change its corporate title upon reorganization.

After emerging from the receivership, and riding on a tide of postwar economic development in the region which it served, Frisco immediately embarked upon a rapid dieselization program, which was essentially complete by the end of 1951. With expansion in mind, it purchased the Alabama, Tennessee & Northern RR in 1948, securing permanent access to the Port of Mobile which had depended upon a close operating agreement with the AT&N dating to 1928. A serious attempt to acquire control of the Central of Georgia was rebuffed by the Interstate Commerce Commission, and thereafter the Frisco settled down to securing maximum benefit from the property as it stood in 1955.

From the mid-Fifties until the end of independent existence, the Frisco operated the "X" main lines as fast freight properties, while the various branches and lighter-traffic lines were judiciously employed to feed the mains. Two connecting short lines were acquired when the time seemed propitious: North East Oklahoma in 1964, and Okmulgee Northern later the same year. Motive power purchases are outlined in roster form elsewhere in this book, and operating practices over the diesel years are noted in photo captions and comments throughout. When Burlington Northern assumed control at the end of 1980, it inherited a company whose roots extend back to the very beginning of railroading in St. Louis.

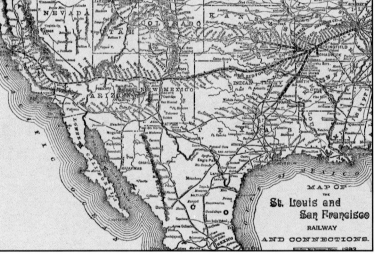

MAP OF THE St. Louis and San Francisco RAILWAY AND CONNECTIONS.

FRISCO STEAM

In Receivership since 1933, the Frisco managed to find the funds to rebuilt ancient 2-10-2's into two series of modern 4-8-2's. They came in the nick of time; wartime traffic very nearly buried the road under an avalanche of tonnage. One of these, the 4419, is the subject of this remarkable panorama of a railroad at war, taken from atop a boxcar in the Springfield yards in the winter of 1944-45. The train is standing on the approximate site of the later Diesel Shop, and is headed West. *(M. Morrow/Dischinger Collection)*

(Above) Since the Frisco was essentially dieselized by 1951, there are not many good color photos of steam power in action. Though technically standing still, 4-8-4 4522 on a westbound Train #33 at Aurora, MO in 1943 will just have to do for an action shot of the Frisco during World War II. The engine is brand new, and the "Frisco Fast Freight" fireball on the tender is a concession wrung from a stingy War Production Board.

(M. Morrow/Dischinger Collection)

(Below) The first two 4-8-4's on the Frisco were oil burners specially painted to power the premier METEOR, matching its blue and white rolling stock. The ready track at Monett, MO in the Spring of 1945 plays host to the 4500, whose accumulation of boiler compound around the blowdown muffler offers mute testimony to the exigencies of wartime traffic.

(M. Morrow/Dischinger Collection)

THE Firefly

KANSAS CITY • TULSA • OKLAHOMA CITY

This photo is unlabelled in its original state but was evidently taken in Memphis sometime before late 1946. It shows one of the splendid 4-6-4's rebuilt by Springfield Shops from large 4-6-2's in the late Thirties. The semi-streamlining and blue paint were intended to match the pre-war blue and white paint scheme of premier trains. The 4-8-4 version of this paint is illustrated earlier. *(J. Schmidt/Peterson Collection)*

The 1500-class 4-8-2's were nearly legendary in their time, equally at home on fast passenger trains and redball freights. Even in postwar no-frills paint (none of the gold pinstriping of its glory days), the 1518 at rest next to the venerable Monett, MO roundhouse in 1948 is still a formidable machine, and obviously in superb mechanical condition.

(M. Morrow/Dischinger Collection)

(Above) In the summer of 1948, Gov. Thomas E. Dewey of New York campaigned for the Presidency against the incumbent, Harry S. Truman of Independence, MO. Carrying its message deep into Truman territory, the Dewey Campaign Special rolls through Logan, MO behind groomed 4-8-2 1515.

(M. Morrow/Dischinger Collection)

(Below) In the steam era, Frisco made extensive use of 2-8-2's for medium-duty road freights. An excellent example is 4136 at North Yard in Springfield. Its top-mounted air reservoirs forecast the "torpedo boat" GP35's delivered some twenty years after this circa 1944 exposure. (M. Morrow/Dischinger Collection)

FRISCO SWITCHERS

(INCLUDING RS-1s)

As with many other Class One railroads, the Frisco sampled 44-ton diesel switchers when the unions agreed that they could be operated without firemen. But Frisco found along with everyone else that the little centercabs were just too light for most work. Whatever its limitations, a Ft. Smith-shopped 44-tonner was a sight to behold. Little GE 44-tonner #7 is basking in the August sun in 1962, sporting new white canvas awnings as well as a new paint job. *(Louis A. Marre)*

(Above) In June of 1963, Emery Gulash chanced upon the Seven Spot actually performing revenue work in Tulsa. The "Full Crew" laws then in effect severely taxed the facilities of a 44-tonner's minuscule cab. Besides this one unit usually assigned to Tulsa, there were two in Ft. Smith (normally in storage there), two in Hugo, OK, one at Wichita, KS and one at Enid, OK. Some were also leased out from time to time to Pullman-Standard in Birmingham and Foreman Cement in Arkansas. *(E. Gulash)*

(Right) Riding a turntable built to accept USRA 2-8-2's, 44-ton GE #8 poses at Ft. Smith in June, 1962. It was in fact carried on the accounts of the Kansas City, Ft. Scott & Memphis (along with 4-8-4's) but that is not marked anywhere on the unit itself. All Frisco 44-tonners did, however, carry unusual "SL-SF" lettering under their road numbers - even when, as in this case, it was not even true. And Quanah, Acme & Pacific lettering on the long hoods of GP-7's was pure fiction. So much for consistency. *(Louis A. Marre)*

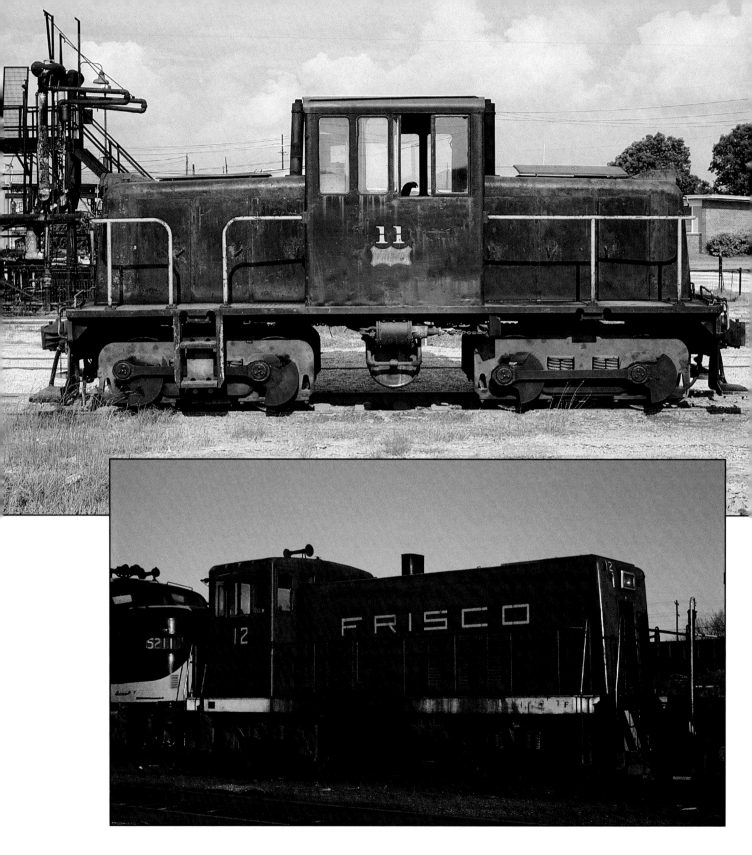

(Top) After the last 44-ton centercabs disappeared, the smallest locomotive remaining on the Frisco was 45-tonner #11, acquired along with the Alabama, Tennessee & Northern in 1948. The little AT&N unit spent its entire life on Blakely Island in Mobile Bay, working the carfloat operation there. It is shown in that location on May 22, 1979, out of service and waiting for a purchaser. Note the frame-mounted brake cylinders and rod-connected wheel sets. The 45-tonner had one traction motor per truck rather than two smaller ones on the 44-tonners. *(Gregory J. Sommers)*

(Bottom) Long after the would-be number twelve vanished before achieving rostered status, Frisco finally acquired a real number 12, also by purchase of a short line, and also a General Electric product. Along with the Okmulgee Northern purchase of August 12, 1964 came 70-tonner #7. Frisco logically assigned it to the next highest small GE number, and so a real 12-spot was lettered and numbered - but not fully repainted. In the year that it was on the road, #12 remained in blue and white with yellow lettering. It worked briefly at Lindenwood and perhaps Tulsa, but was no more adequate than the 44-tonners. This photo shows it awaiting sale at Springfield on Jan. 3, 1965. *(Louis A. Marre)*

Frisco narrowly missed rostering an 80-ton GE when it acquired the Alabama, Tennessee & Northern in 1948. In addition to its 45-tonner (which did last on the Frisco until 1979) and its eleven RS-1's, AT&N had one 80-tonner, #12. It was built in 1942 and joined the other wartime diesels in helping AT&N keep up with the Port of Mobile's war traffic. Frisco sold the unit in 1948, so pictures of it are exceedingly rare. Thank Richard Kindig for (A) finding Kodachrome in 1944, and (B) using some of it on AT&N 12 next to the freight house in Mobile on January 9.

(R.H. Kindig)

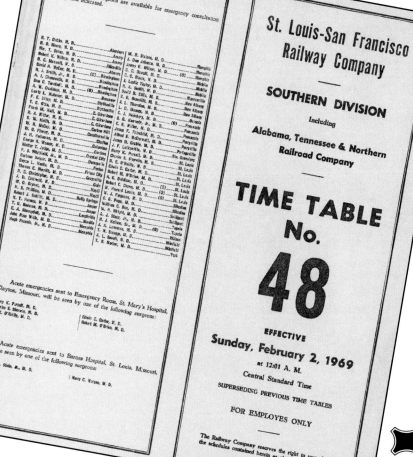

(Above) Along with the Alabama, Tennessee & Northern purchase in 1948 Frisco acquired eleven RS-1's, a model otherwise unrepresented on its roster. These retained "AT&N" sublettering, as the road's corporate identity was not abolished until 1971, two years after the last RS-1 had perished. The "class unit" switches the MoPac interchange at Hoxie, AR on March 31, 1962.

(R.R. Wallin)

(Left) All of the AT&N RS-1's were built with multiple-unit connections on the short hood ends, making two-unit sets possible. From all available photographic evidence, Frisco rarely if ever seems to have made use of this capability, though the apparatus remained visibly in place. This short-end view of freshly-painted 109 outside the Springfield Diesel Shop on February 3, 1961, clearly shows the jumper cable receptacle in the Vee of the handrail brace - but no cable. Did it ever happen? (Marre Collection)

(Right) The RS-1 is, by design, not much more than a 1000 h.p. switcher hood on a frame elongated just enough to add a short hood. AT&N 102 switches Lindenwood on May 1, 1965.

(Mike Condren)

(Below) As a true roadswitcher, AT&N 111 is working a Monett, MO to Rogers, AR local on July 11, 1963, and is here seen shuffling an SP boxcar in feed grain service around the poultry feed mill district in Springdale, AR. (Louis A. Marre)

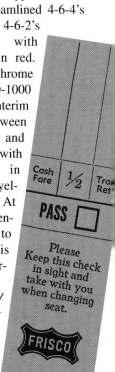

(Above) Frisco's first wartime Baldwin switchers came in a blue and white version of the passenger paint scheme (also applied to two 4-8-4's, semi-streamlined 4-6-4's and the "Firefly" 4-6-2's and trainsets) with "Frisco Lines" in red. This early Kodachrome of 1945-built VO-1000 226 shows an interim paint scheme between blue and white and solid black: blue, with "Frisco Lines" in white (perhaps yellow) on the hood. At least one 44-ton centercab is likely to have shared this short-lived appearance as well.

(M. Morrow/ Dischinger Collection)

Whatever her body color in 1945, VO-1000 226 lasted long enough to go through the black era and get a mandarin orange and white update in 1967. The result more or less glows in the dark at Ft. Smith on the 21st. of December in that year. The unit stayed in this gaudy dress until traded-in to EMD in April, 1972 for a GP38-2. *(Louis A. Marre)*

(Above) The standard switcher assignment to the Central Division Shop in Ft. Smith was, for many years, the VO-1000. One example, the redoubtable 213, will go to work there just as soon as the business meeting on its front steps is adjourned. From this September 5, 1961 date, the Baldwin era has just a decade remaining: the last six were retired in April 1972, but had been out of service since late in 1971. (Louis A. Marre)

(Right) "Look, Daddy, a too-too twain!" "No, son, I think it's a too-too-too twain." Is the Fayetteville switcher on September 24, 1963 obeying the traffic light or his conductor's hand signals?

(Mike Condren)

(Above) In his indefatigable travels, the peripatetic Elliott Kahn encountered this vision in mandarin orange outside the Ft. Smith roundhouse late in the afternoon of August 12, 1970. Baldwin rumblings were stilled forever on Frisco property just a bit over one year later. (Elliott Kahn)

(Below) Baldwin's VO production ran through a mind-boggling gamut of exhaust system arrangements, and the two-stacked version was by far the rarest. Frisco 228, whose passenger station chores at Springfield on December 22, 1967 are illustrated, is one of the two-stacked variety. It could in some circumstances be confused with Frisco's two-stacked EMD repowerings; but it is a pure Baldwin product. (Louis A. Marre)

(Above) It may have been because they were more often in the shop, but Frisco's Baldwin, Alco and Fairbanks - Morse switchers always looked spiffy. Case in point: VO-1000 219 at Kansas City on March 24, 1967. Its round Baldwin builder's plate is clearly visible on the frame just above the "F" mark. (R.R. Wallin)

(Below) The 236 is a VO-1000 of the four-stacked persuasion. Its reflective yellow striping has a near-holographic dimensional effect in this Springfield scene of Christmas eve-eve, 1967. (Louis A. Marre)

(Above) Baldwin purchases outlasted the VO-generation by a mere four units: DS4-4-1000's 238-241 of December 1948. Though the VO's worked system-wide, the DS's stayed in Springfield virtually from delivery to disposition. The 241 was there, as usual, on July 8, 1962. *(Louis A. Marre)*

(Above) Everybody who had one longed to repower a VO, and many did. The Frisco tried out the idea on nine of their forty, decided that the result was not worth the expense, and soldiered on with the remainder for the full twenty years and more of their equipment trusts. Repowered with an EMD 12-567 at the La Grange IL plant of the builder, the first three were done in 1957, the last six in 1959. The latter had multiple unit capacity installed as well. Frisco 205, of the first batch, with a plywood sheet on the front and the switchman on the rear, waits at Springfield station for the WILL ROGERS on December 28, 1964. *(Louis A. Marre)*

(Right) A cold and gray February 6, 1979 finds and EMD-repowered Baldwin switcher between chores in the Springfield yard. Repowered in 1959, the 206 departed from the roster six months after this interlude in a busy life. One of the second-round repowerings, it has MU added.

(Gregory J. Sommers)

(Below) Frisco's NW-2's worked for more than thirty years for their first owner, and at one time or another were found on almost every part of the system. In October of 1964 a pair are serviced and ready at Lindenwood. Their original "railroad Roman" style lettering is still in place. *(R.R. Wallin)*

(Above) Since their longevity extended even past the end of Frisco's corporate identity, the NW-2's were all eventually converted to the mandarin orange image. Still in St. Louis, the transmogrified 254 has a repainted Wide Vision caboose for backdrop in this May 12, 1979 version of the 1964 photo just preceding.

(Gregory J. Sommers)

(Left) The placid course of a lowly NW-2's existence has been rudely interrupted, and the result waits outside the Diesel Shop on April 28, 1966 for some estimates. The damage was not fatal: see the view of 265 many years later, just below.

(Louis A. Marre)

(Right) First-generation diesel switcher purchases rounded out with ten SW-7s in 1950/51 and five SW-9's in 1952. All of the SW-7's, and just one of the SW-9's came without MU connections. The redoubtable 304, last and greatest of the SW-7's, waits for Christmas on December 23, 1967, at the Shops in Springfield.

(Louis A. Marre)

FRISCO

ST. LOUIS-SAN FRANCISCO
RAILWAY COMPANY

PASSENGER TRAIN
SCHEDULES

(Right) Sooner or later, every Frisco unit visited the backshop in Springfield, MO. Thirty-year-old NW-2 265 is doing so in the cold wind of February 5, 1979. When the work is finished, the unit will return to its Tulsa assignment. It shows no trace of the mishap in 1966 documented in the previous view.

(Gregory J. Sommers)

(Left) SW-9 306 and brake sled X80 rumble into view in the yard at Memphis on a steaming July 23, 1962. The MU apparatus and folding walkway are clearly visible on the front of the unit. (Louis A. Marre)

(Below) Although the mandarin orange and white paint scheme dates to February 14, 1965, many units remained in black and yellow for over a decade thereafter. Most were GP-7's destined for retirement, but some "keepers" remained in black until an aggressive program to repaint them started in 1977. A late survivor of the previous standard is SW-9 310 shown here in St. Louis in June, 1977. (Gregory J. Sommers)

(Above) Tennessee Yard, in Capleville, TN just East of Memphis, is whitened by two inches of snow on this February 7, 1979. While this is not a substantial snowfall by some standards, it has virtually paralyzed Memphis. The yard is fully functional, and SW-9's 308 and 309 are tackling another cut of cars. The major problem is a crew shortage; nobody can negotiate the treacherous highways, as very little snow removal equipment is on the road.
(Gregory J. Sommers)

(Below) Five SW-7 and ten SW-9 switchers from Electro-Motive completed the Frisco's initial dieselization program by 1952. No more switchers were needed until the Alco, Baldwin and Fairbanks-Morse fleet reached the end of economic life. The last first-generation switcher, SW-9 314, works Tennessee Yard in November of 1973, still in black paint. It was the only SW-9 bought without multiple unit control, for some reason lost to history. *(Gregory J. Sommers)*

(Above) The Frisco could afford neither repowering nor early retirement of its minority 16-unit Fairbanks-Morse switcher stable, so it chose the next best option and kept it at Tulsa, where its mechanics soon learned to speak Opposed Piston fluently. In the bright noontime of Tulsa on July 1, 1962, an elegant set of examples pauses briefly between chores.

(Louis A. Marre)

(Left) Liberally-striped H10-44 272 has grabbed a venerable outside-braced wooden boxcar in the Tulsa yard in June, 1964, and is preparing to pull a cut. Since all F-M switchers worked out of Tulsa, the little shop there was able to keep them in immaculate condition.

(E. Gulash)

Frisco's black and yellow switcher image and its post-1964 mandarin orange and white image may be graphically contrasted by reference to these two views of the same unit, H10-44 275. The black image is at Tulsa on July 1, 1962, and the orange one at the same location on May 10, 1970. *(Louis A. Marre) (Owen Leander)*

(Right) Fairbanks switchers lasted just long enough to share in the orange painting fever. The new image has been only recently applied to the 271, shown here in Oklahoma City on July 31, 1968. The marker lamps on the front indicate that a stint of local freight work rather than mundane switching is in the offing. (Wm. C. Pletz)

(Below) The Final Four F-M's were H12-44's, but kept the cab roof overhang carbody characteristic of all H10-44 production. They came with cab-end multiple unit connections, and were used in pairs on the Cherokee Yard hump until displaced by SW1500's, those in turn replaced by SD38-2's. The 284-285 set is just attacking another cut to be wrestled around with 2400 horses on July 1, 1962. That first car is one of the original tri-levels.

(Louis A. Marre)

(Above) Cherokee Yard's hump is a "hold-back" rather than solely a "push" arrangement, so it requires as much braking power as tractive effort from its engines. Before the dynamic-braked SD38-2's were acquired, Frisco built three "brake sleds" from steam locomotive tenders specifically to provide more brake power for this hump (and for heavy transfers in Memphis). One of these is working along with a pair of Fairbanks-Morse switchers in Tulsa in 1960. The H10-44 in the middle, the 281, was retrofitted with multiple unit control by Frisco so as to have one spare on hand in the event of mishap to one of the four H12-44's bought originally with MU.

(E. Gulash)

(Left) One of the bought-new Alco switchers (four more came with the North East Oklahoma RR in 1964) has found a home in Memphis as of July 19, 1962. Its de-cabbed sibling 292B is working on the hump at this same time. The other three were usually assigned to Springfield. *(Louis A. Marre)*

(Above) Alco S-2 292 lost its cab in a collision in 1958, and became a booster unit more or less permanently mated to an SW-9 on the Tennessee Yard hump. it is seen here in that role on July 19, 1962, framed by a set of road power on its way to the diesel house, led by F-7A 5022.

(Louis A. Marre)

(Left) After Frisco purchased the North East Oklahoma outright on Jan. 14, 1964, it continued to operate the property with the Alco switchers which came with the deal. On May 7, 1966, S-2 297 is still switching its original habitat in Miami, OK, wearing a Frisco number but still painted and lettered NEO. *(Louis A. Marre)*

(Above) The Alco switchers which came along with the North East Oklahoma purchase in 1964 nearly doubled the Frisco fleet of such units. They remained in their original livery until retired as a group in 1972. At some point, they were restencilled merely "SL-SF" above their numbers, and that was all the repainting they ever enjoyed. Ex-NEO's now SL-SF 296 and 297 share the Lindenwood sand track with black NW-2 256 on November 11, 1967. (R.R. Wallin)

(Right) Frisco's only S-4 model switcher, ex-NEO 706, became SL-SF 298. Carrying exactly that label, "SL-SF 298" it is shown here working in multiple with sibling S-2 297 on original North East Oklahoma property at Miami, OK on October 26, 1968.

(Elliott Kahn)

(Above) The largest yard switcher class on the property was occupied by forty-six SW1500's. In June, 1974 the 350 is working Springfield industrial spurs, one of the usual chores for these useful little machines.
(Gregory J. Sommers)

(Below) The first two SW1500's, 316 and 315, catch the early morning light at Tennessee Yard on May 25, 1979. When new some eleven years previous, they ushered in a new era for yard power on the Frisco. By the time deliveries were completed in 1973, all Baldwin, Alco and Fairbanks-Morse switchers had been retired. (Gregory J. Sommers)

(Above) All major Frisco yards were assigned SW1500's, and those assignments tended not to change very often. In St. Louis, one regular duty was the Valley Park Turn, to serve the Chrysler assembly plant there. A morning and an afternoon turn delivered auto parts cars and empty auto racks, primarily from Norfolk & Western and Penn Central, and brought out finished autos. Here, 323 and 324 await the 3:00 Turn outside the Lindenwood house in June, 1974. (Gregory J. Sommers)

(Below) The car repair track at Amory, MS is under the care of SW1500 325 on May 20, 1979. Amory is still a crew change point at this time, but not much more. In times past, it had a roundhouse and small diesel shop. Some early orange and white repaintings were done there. The Consolidated Mechanical Shops at Springfield were just what the title says, and all small shops were closed in the late Sixties. Outdoor repair-in-place tracks for minor car repairs remained, however, in locations large and small - hence this scene.

(Gregory J. Sommers)

(Top) Compared to an SW1500, the MP15 is five feet longer, a difference readily apparent in this view of MP15 362 and SW1500 329. After purchasing a total of 46 SW1500's, Frisco ordered only five MP15DC's, all built in March 1975. The extra cost of the elongated switcher was less effective than making a slightly larger investment but getting a true roadswitcher, and so Frisco moved to the GP15-1 and bought twenty-five. By the time of this May 1979 photo, the five MP15's had all gathered in Birmingham. *(Gregory J. Sommers)*

(Bottom) In June 1974, two-year-old SW1500 349 and caboose 1205 await the return of a crew at Springfield Yard. Although Springfield Yard was the center of the "X" of Frisco main lines, it was not a hump yard - only Tulsa and Memphis were of that size. Springfield had a "poor man's hump," i.e. a slight rise in the West end of the yard which somewhat facilitated switching from that end.

(Gregory J. Sommers)

A Green Light 🚦 *for Economy in Railroad Operation*

(Right and below) The last Frisco switcher came from used locomotive dealer Precision National Corp. in 1979. An SW-1 #10 replaced 45-ton GE #11 in Mobile. It had been built in 1941 for Great Northern, and subsequently worked for Burlington Northern on its Walla Walla Valley subsidiary. Two views on May 22, 1979 show the "new" switcher both with and without the idler flatcar which it used to load and unload the Blakely Island barge traffic without getting the locomotive itself on the barges. Upon the merger of Frisco into the BN in November 1980, this unit "returned to its roots."

(Gregory J. Sommers)

FRISCO ROAD PASSENGER UNITS

[E7/8]

(Left and above) The May, 1948 demonstration tour of the new Pullman-Standard lightweight METEOR consist was recorded fully by the Company photographer only in black and white. Fortunately, the switch crew which moved the train to the Shops in Springfield included amateur photographer Millard Morrow. Here are the only known color views of the absolutely new train, E-7A 2005 leading, in its original stainless steel trim which it would lose in 1950 when it was made over to look like the new E-8A's. The METEOR trainset probably never was completely matched again as it is here, since there were not enough head-end lightweight cars for full service. (M. Morrow/Dischinger Collection)

(Above) After only two years in TEXAS SPECIAL livery, the E-7's were repainted and re-trimmed to match the new E-8's of 1950. At the same time, they were each named after a famous horse - mostly racing horses, but not entirely. The number and name list is printed in the accompanying table. The earliest color view that could be located after the change of image is this juxta-position of 2002 *Comanche* outshining NYC E-8 4079 on St. Louis Union Station service tracks in August of 1953. Note the white separation line between the gold trim and the red body color. *(Joe Collias)*

(Above) Shortly before 5:30 PM on July 17, 1948, a pair of Frisco E-7's stands crewed and ready for the advertised departure of the TEXAS SPECIAL from St. Louis. The 2003 and an unidentifiable mate are one-third of Frisco's 1947 order. MKT contributed a train set and a fourth pair of E-7's in similar paint. Besides the train name in script, each unit assigned to the train carried the heralds of both companies, and a blue lone star on the nose door. (R.T. Fillman)

(Left) In its days of glory, the TEXAS SPECIAL boasted of through sleeping car service between its main Texas points and New York, Chicago, and Washington (via PRR, Wabash and B&O respectively) in addition to the St. Louis sleepers. But MKT did not have sufficient time to turn the train at San Antonio on many occasions, and so the original pair of Pullman-Standard lightweight trains (one MKT, one SL-SF) shortly had to be supplemented by repainted heavyweight equipment for a third trainset. In 1955, a re-order of lightweight coaches and one extra coach-buffet-lounge eased the shortage, but there were never enough head-end lightweights and observations to go around. This panorama of the Eastbound train leaving Dallas in August of 1951 clearly shows the B&O and PRR cars in their respective liveries. The Wabash sleeper is missing. Several red and silver repainted heavyweight cars are also in evidence. The green MKT RPO-express car is testimony to the lack of matching head-end equipment. Be that as it may, a glittering team of E-8's has matters firmly in hand, with *Messenger* 2008 in the lead. (R.S. Plummer)

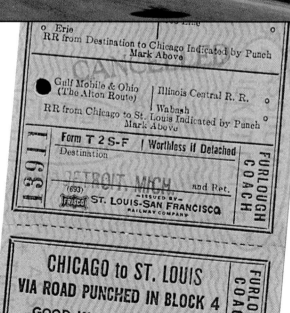

Comanche shows the simpler post-1960 image on the head of the KANSAS CITY - FLORIDA SPECIAL at Kansas City on July 15, 1962. Long considered secondary to the St. Louis - Texas service, this route in fact outlasted the other and saw the end of all Frisco passenger service in November of 1967. *(Frank Tatnall)*

(Above) The white separating stripe which highlighted the gold trim on the named E-units proved very difficult to maintain. In 1960 the painting diagram was altered and this detail omitted. *Winchester* has just received the latest image at Springfield on October 28, 1961.

(R.R. Wallin)

(Below) *Whirlaway* aka 2007 and 2009 stand apart from the METEOR consist in Oklahoma City on April 14, 1964. By this date, the revised painting diagram calls for solid red with a yellow nose patch ... and no name.

(J.B. McCall)

(Above) "All change at Springfield!" Though passengers might not need to, passenger power changed at Springfield. Seen from street level, 2006 is involved in power swap for the WILL ROGERS in October of 1965. A single E is stashed in the siding on the left, and another's nose is visible in the background. One of the reasons for this power dance is the presence of the System Diesel Shop - where horses can be watered, fed, and washed.

(Louis A. Marre)

December, 1952

FRISCO

MISSOURI..
KANSAS...
ARKANSAS
OKLAHOMA
TEXAS.....
TENNESSEE.
MISSISSIPPI
ALABAMA..
FLORIDA...

5000 MILES
IN NINE STATES

(Below) Without its horse name and in the last modification of the red and yellow paint scheme, E-8 2011 and an E-7 mate stand in front of the venerable Birmingham station on February 6, 1965, awaiting the KANSAS CITY - FLORIDA SPECIAL departure.

(Gordon E. Lloyd)

.....Diesel Powered.....

THE METEOR

STREAMLINER BETWEEN
St. Louis-Tulsa-Oklahoma City
Berths, Roomettes, Bedrooms
Compartments, Drawing-rooms
Dining and Lounge Cars
Chair-Lounge-Buffet Car

TEXAS SPECIAL

STREAMLINER BETWEEN
St. Louis-Dallas-Ft. Worth and San Antonio
Berths, Roomettes, Bedrooms
and Drawing-rooms
Dining and Lounge Cars
Chair-Lounge-Buffet Car

THRU SLEEPING CARS
Between NEW YORK-WASHINGTON and TEXAS

KANSAS CITY-FLORIDA SPECIAL

BETWEEN
Kansas City and
the Southeast
Streamlined Sleepers,
Berths, Roomettes, Bed-
rooms and Compartments
THRU TO FLORIDA
LOUNGE AND DINING CARS
STREAMLINED RECLINING SEAT CHAIR CARS

The all-stops local on the St. Louis - Oklahoma City run for thirty years was the WILL ROGERS. It is shown here making its Rolla, MO pause on October 11, 1965. More freight than passenger, its head-end cars out-number its occupied ones by a two-to-one ratio. *(Louis A. Marre)*

(Above) Secondary passenger trains on the Frisco were usually powered either with steam generator GP-7's or, more often, with an FP-7. Most non-streamlined rolling stock remained Pullman green, so the black and yellow freight colors of these units made an agreeable match. An occasional stray E-unit on these little trains put a crimson exclamation mark upon their mundane consists, as 2009 is doing at the head of four-car #710 - the Ft. Smith, Arkansas METEOR connection - on June 16, 1961. *Jet Pilot* on the engine is a bad omen: airline service to St. Louis killed this train. *(Louis A. Marre)*

(Below) Even the mighty KANSAS CITY - FLORIDA SPECIAL deigned to stop at tiny Amory, MS because it is the crew change point between Memphis and Birmingham. On July 20, 1962, with 2011 *Gallant Fox* and 2012 *Flying Ebony*, it is doing just that. The lead unit is in "old" paint, the trailing in "new" at this date. *(Louis A. Marre)*

(Above) The "old paint/new paint" distinction begun with the simplification of the striping in 1960 rapidly degenerated into "latest" as passenger service dwindled with increasing rapidity. Before the last-minute change to orange and white, there were some units painted in a red and yellow version of the simplified freight black and yellow: no side stripes at all, no names, and a yellow (not gold) "patch" on the nose. Nameless 2006 in storage at Springfield on December 23, 1967 is a good example. It was traded-in to EMD in October of the following year. (Louis A. Marre)

BETWEEN
ST. LOUIS
SPRINGFIELD
TULSA
OKLAHOMA CITY
DIESEL-POWERED, STREAMLINED

THE
OKLAHOMAN

RECLINING CHAIR CAR
CHAIR-LOUNGE-BUFFET CAR

BETWEEN
KANSAS CITY
SPRINGFIELD
MEMPHIS
BIRMINGHAM
DIESEL-POWERED, STREAMLINED

THE
SOUTHLAND

RECLINING CHAIR CAR
CHAIR-LOUNGE-BUFFET CAR
SLEEPING CAR

(Below) An incongruous match is Count Fleet and a lowly FP-7, but #710's consist is inflated with four business cars of a Director's inspection on July 12, 1963, and so the Ft. Smith train goes big time. (Mike Condren)

FRISCO

Serving: MISSOURI • KANSAS • ARKANSAS • OKLAHOMA • TEXAS
TENNESSEE • MISSISSIPPI • ALABAMA • FLORIDA

(Right) Before the completion of Tennessee Yard in far suburban Capleville, TN, Frisco's Memphis terminal struggled with four small yards scattered from the Arkansas side of the Mississippi eastward. In the West Memphis yard on September 24, 1954, E-8's 2017 and 2013 have come back across the Memphis bridge for servicing. With this view, we begin a series of episodes in the life of *Pensive*.

(Marvin H. Cohen)

(Below) The second installment of *Pensive* adventures is this scene on New Year's Day, 1967. Service has dropped to one train on each main, and 2017 is leading the SOUTHLAND through Lenexa, KS with an amazing amount of head-end traffic, plus an ominous residue of passenger equipment.

(Don Ball Collection)

(Above) Redoubtable 2017 drew the melancholy assignment which took the last Frisco passenger train out of St. Louis. The final Westbound OKLAHOMAN catches the last rays of daylight in Kirkwood May 14, 1967. The consist is predominantly green, and we see it from both ends. The rear is punctuated by lightweight coach-buffet-lounge *Sterling Price* still in good order albeit with a black (rather than red) roof.

(Joe Collias)

(Left) Six E-units were sufficient to cover the one train remaining in the last half of 1967, and 2017 was one of them. It was one of three repainted in July with the mandarin orange and white image. Shown waiting for the power change at Springfield in August (with 2020) it looks wholly incongrous in its last gaudy image. If it foresaw its fate, no wonder it was *Pensive* for most of its career: it happened to be on the very last Frisco passenger train. *(Joe Collias)*

(Below) *Comanche* 2019 and a stablemate have brought the sole Frisco passenger train into its Springfield crew and engine change point on the same day on which the 2017-2020 set is shown earlier. The SOUTH-LAND is indistinguishable from a mail and express train at this angle, and indeed it is not much else. Six or seven E-units are sufficient for the needs of this one train, and eleven of the 23 are already off the property. By October 1968 all were gone. This vestigial train expired on December 8th of 1967. *(Joe Collias)*

Both ends of the METEOR during its Oklahoma City layover of New Years Eve 1962 are shown here. The consist lacks an observation lounge, but all the occupied cars are lightweight, stream-lined, and in good matching paint. Power for the day is the customary E-8 pair, in this instance 2018 *Ponder* and 2012 *Flying Ebony. (J.B. McCall)*

West of Oklahoma City, the METEOR ran as an abbreviated train (one RPO, one baggage, one coach, one sleeper) out to Lawton, OK, to provide service to Fort Sill. The full complement of two E-8's is hardly necessary on this December morning in 1960 as the train leaves Oklahoma City, but it was easier to take them as a pair than to break them up and re-connect them on the return to the full consist for the Eastbound train in the evening. *(Collection of E. Gulash)*

The Twilight of the Gods. The METE-OR, once the premier train of the Frisco, flickered off the timetable on September 17, 1965, taking its Ft. Smith connecting train with it. On August 26th, with less than a month remaining to run, #9 makes its customary halt at the crew change point of Monett, MO. The 2018 is the lead unit on this warm and still evening, its exhaust rising almost straight up into the darkness.

(Mike Condren)

they're **ALL*** aboard Frisco's

KANSAS CITY—FLORIDA SPECIAL

⭐ the passenger who wants the peaceful privacy of his own *bedroom*.

⭐ the passenger who desires the deep-sleep invitation of a *roomette*.

⭐ the passenger who appreciates the head-to-toe comfort and economy of a *reclining chair car*.

⭐ the passenger who seeks the walk-around freedom and companionship of the *lounge car*.

...they're looking for comfort...that's why they're aboard!

FRISCO'S KANSAS CITY—FLORIDA SPECIAL, with all passenger carrying cars lightweight and streamlined, takes them all aboard...gives a holiday atmosphere the moment you step aboard.

Here are other luxuries: delicious meals; friendly service and hospitality; smooth, Diesel-powered ride. If you're traveling Southeast, try FRISCO'S KANSAS CITY—FLORIDA SPECIAL. All this is aboard.

FOR SCHEDULES AND EQUIPMENT, SEE TABLES 4 AND 7

53

FRISCO ROAD FREIGHT UNITS

(F3/7/9 FP7 FA FB)

Road freight dieselization was handled with the type of diesels considered most appropriate at the time, i.e. 1500 hp cabs and boosters, from both Electro-Motive and American Locomotive. In the first big push, the two builders had a nearly equal share: 34 F-3 and F-7A with 24 matching boosters vs. 32 FA-1 and 16 boosters. The 244-engined FA/FB's proved costly to maintain, and from 1950 onward only EMD's of similar models were purchased. The F-3 and F-7 fleet was rounded out with F9B's, some as late as 1957. In the siding a Logan, MO, 23 miles west of Springfield on the main line to Oklahoma, a matched set of F-3's with 5009 in the lead waits for a meet. It is the Spring of 1950, and the units are just two years old. By the end of 1951, dieselization will be complete for all road trains. *(M. Morrow/Dischinger Collection)*

(Above) The F-3's were purchased in A-B-B-A sets and long operated in exactly that configuration. The 5010 and companions are shown here in the old diesel service area in Springfield just before construction of the Diesel Shop at the end of 1949. Note the lack of any MU arrangements on the nose, the plain unlettered B-units, no painted number on the A-unit below the cab: these are in as-delivered condition. (M. Morrow/Dischinger Collection)

(Below) Once the novelty wore off, F-units of any model worked in multiple, and front-end MU capacity was retrofitted to the A-units for greater flexibility in making combinations. By September 14, 1962, 1948-built F-3A 5003 has made the change, as shown by this view in Springfield. (Louis A. Marre)

(*Above*) Unthinkable in 1950, but Standard Operating Practice a decade later, an "F-Unit Sandwich" awaits the call for #730 outside the Ft. Smith, AR roundhouse on June 28, 1963: F-3A 5008, three GP-7's, and another F-3A all in multiple. (*Louis A. Marre*)

(*Below*) A very mixed bag of cab units drags across the T&P - MKT - ATSF crossing in Tulsa on a muggy June day in 1964. The lead unit is F-3A 5014, fully equipped with front-end MU. It is followed by FP-7 5042, an F-7B, and an EMD repowered FB-1. No more matching sets of same models, to say the least! (*E. Gulash*)

A five-unit F-set in the service track at Tennessee Yard on July 23, 1962 testifies to growing train sizes. A-B-B-A is no longer sufficient. In fact, thirteen additional F9B's were bought in 1954 and 1957 in an attempt to keep up appearances as well as tonnage. There were never enough to go around, so there are four A-units in this consist and a single F7B in the center. *(Louis A. Marre)*

DIESEL POWER
for the greater... FRISCO

The Frisco now has in service or on order 133 Diesel electric road and switching units. These new freight locomotives will hasten shipments between St. Louis, the southeast and southwest . . . Between Kansas City, Memphis, Birmingham and the southeast . . . Between Kansas City, Tulsa, Oklahoma City, Dallas, Fort Worth and points beyond.

(Right) At Tulsa on July 1, 1962 F-7A 5029 shows the good effects of a recent repainting. The full original scheme is still being maintained, which includes a green anti-glare finish on the top of the nose. Front end MU is about the only major modification to this thirteen-year old unit since delivery. *(Louis A. Marre)*

(Below) Frying in the noonday sun of Mississippi, a redball changes crews at Amory on July 20, 1962. At this point in time, air conditioning is for passenger cars. Whoever heard of a comfortable diesel cab? Leading FP-7 5044, two F7B's, and a repowered FA are, in spite of external variety, all chanting the same 1500 hp 567 tune. *(Louis A. Marre)*

(Left) Orange and white paint spread to the F-unit fleet considerably in advance of the renumbering of 1968. A nice example is F-7 5037 at Ft. Smith on December 21, 1967. The legislated spark arrestor bonnets on the exhaust stacks have also participated in the orange repainting.

(Louis A. Marre)

(Below) The Frisco was very quick to see the advantage of a dual-service F-type. In 1950-51, twelve FP-7 units supplemented the F-7 purchases of the same period. From 1950 to 1960 there were still just enough small passenger trains to keep them fully employed (e.g. Tulsa-Enid, Monett-Wichita, Monett-Paris, Amory-Pensacola-Mobile). As these gradually withered away, the units went into freight service without further ado. When all passenger service ended, their steam generators were removed, and that was that. In the black and yellow passenger service era we will look at five examples, all on the METEOR connecting Train #710. Originally a Monett, MO to Paris, TX operation, it was cut back from its Texas terminal to Ft. Smith, AR in 1957. From that point until the end of all service in 1965, an FP-7 was the power of choice - and that one usually the 5047. The first view is, however, the "spare" unit, 5045, standing at the combination depot and Central Division office building in Ft. Smith on September 8, 1961. An FP-7, a baggage car, a baggage-RPO, a coach, and a sleeper for forwarding to St. Louis on the METEOR make up the standard consist. All cars are in green on this day.

(Louis A. Marre)

(Above) With regularly-assigned FP-7 5047 up front, the entire 709-710 train set was regularly turned as a unit after its 6:45 AM arrival from Monett. Still complete, it has turned and points North for its 7:00 PM departure. The train is on the roundhouse service track where 5047's needs will first be attended to on this second day of 1963. (Mike Condren)

(Right) At 7:06 PM on June 28, 1963, Train #710 dusts the northern yard leads with EMD smoke, making a dramatic exit from Ft. Smith. It will arrive in Monett, MO, the junction with the St. Louis main, at 11:25 PM. The sleeper on the rear will be cut in to the eastbound METEOR and depart at 12:45 AM, arriving in St. Louis at 8 AM. Meanwhile, a sleeper from St. Louis on the westbound METEOR will be dropped at 1:05 AM and #709 then depart for Ft. Smith at 2:05, arriving at 6:45. For such a train, an FP-7 is ideal.

(Louis A. Marre)

(Right) Seen from the deserted platform of the Missouri Pacific depot in Ft. Smith, #710 prepares for departure to Monett on June 15, 1964. The imposing Frisco station houses the Central Division offices on its second floor. It was built in 1904 during a period of Rock Island control of the Frisco, when money clearly was no object. The building survives in 1995, long since out of railroad use. The train in front of it pulled out forever on September 17, 1965. *(Louis A. Marre)*

(Below) Before the simultaneous demise of the METEOR and its METEORITE connection to Ft. Smith, the southbound train is seen in the Ft. Smith station on the morning of July 4, 1964. All such scenes ceased on September 17, 1965, leaving only a bus connection to the KCS main line at Sallisaw, OK for "rail" travel out of Ft. Smith. *(Louis A. Marre)*

(Left) Standard appearance for FP-7's in the late black and yellow era included a nose-door second headlight, front-end MU, radio, larger lettering, a painted number beneath the cab windows, no fuel tank skirting, multiple-chime horns, and the nose herald plaque. Our example is 5045, at Ft. Smith on June 16, 1961. *(Louis A. Marre)*

(Below) There were F9B's on the property shortly prior to the remanufacture of F3A's 5005 and 5007 into F9AM's in February of 1954. The "A" units were needed to control the dynamic braking on the "B" units; until that time, no Frisco diesel had that feature. Santa Fe, on the other hand, did have dynamic braking on F-types, and it was the run-through traffic via the QA&P and Santa Fe to Los Angeles that sparked the purchase and rebuilding of units that could be fully compatible with Santa Fe practice. At Oklahoma City in February of 1965, F9AM 5005 leads no fewer than four F9B's and another A unit, turning back West after handing off a Santa Fe train to a new set of power. *(J.B. McCall)*

(Above) Renumbered and repainted into orange and white, three F-units plus a black GP-7 and black F-7 await the call for #731 at Ft. Smith on the day after Christmas in 1970. The Frisco has just a bit less than a decade remaining as an independent entity.

(Louis A. Marre)

(Left) The "big orange" era of repainted F-units was a brief one. Even the F9B's were gone by 1974, and very few of the cab units were around to match up with them in the last couple of years. A nice set at Lindenwood in August of 1972 also demonstrates one of the adverse effects: lead F-7 25, former 5025, and two of the others are spectacularly orange ... but the F3B is very worn black and yellow. A fully-matched orange set was very difficult to assemble.

(Joe Collias)

(Below) West of Springfield, westbound BTX rolls expeditiously behind FP-7 43, four more F's and a single U25B on March 18, 1972. The lead FP-7 was sold for scrap in October of 1974. *(Edward Kanak)*

Noted St. Louis photographer Joe Collias observed Train #33 rolling through Kirkwood on April 14, 1973 with a matched quartet of orange F units. Knowing that the F-unit era was very near its end on the Frisco, he chased the train West, and the results included two splendid views of the period: just West of Cuba, MO in a rock cut, and passing the St. James, MO depot at full speed. *(Joe Collias)*

(Left) By the time of this June 1974 slice of action in Springfield, the Frisco fleet of "covered wagon" units was down to a mere handful of active numbers. Thus the odds for a matched A-B-B-A set were very low; but behold F-7A 34, F-9B 138, F-7B 118 and F-3A 62 arriving with Train #730 from Ft. Smith, AR. All four were retired by November of this same year and sold to Precision National Corp. for dismantling. (Gregory J. Sommers)

(Below) The EMD repowered FA/FB Alco freight units lasted a bit longer than their as-built kin, but not much longer. They were in practice just another F unit if they had EMD prime movers inside. The 5203 leads two GP-7's, a repowered FB, and an F7A on Train #731 through the depot at Fayetteville, AR on March 12, 1964. (Mike Condren)

The Frisco had never been a very big Alco customer even in the days of steam. Its experience with Alco's diesel production was limited to five RS-2's, nine S-2/S-4 switchers (four of these secondhand along with the North East Oklahoma in 1964), the eleven RS-1's inherited with the Alabama, Tennessee & Northern purchase of 1948, and enough FA-1 and FB-1 road freight units in 1948-49 to make sixteen A-B-A sets. The 244-model prime movers in the RS-2/FA series proved very expensive to maintain, and the RS-2's were repowered with EMD engines. A similar program was undertaken for the cab units, but was so expensive that 18 of them were left as Alco had built them. They were, however, stored as often as traffic would allow, and used sparingly when in service. Two of the as-built examples are illustrated here during rare guest appearances on the road: 5231 at Rosedale Yard in Kansas City, KS on June 16, 1961, and 5210 outside the Diesel Shop (a very familiar location for it) on July 9, 1962. A few repowered FB's lasted long enough to get three-digit numbers in 1968, but all FA/FB types, whatever their prime mover, were gone by September 1969. None were repainted in orange and white.

(R.R. Wallin) (Louis A. Marre)

Frisco's standard black and yellow freight livery suited Alco carbody units very nicely. As proof, the left side of 5207 at Kansas City in June of 1962 and the right side of 5217 at Tulsa in July of 1961 are offered here. A stan-

dard EMD badge builder's plate was affixed just above the original cast iron Alco rectangular plate to denote repowering at La Grange in February 1956 and August 1955 respectively. *(Louis A. Marre)*

None of the FA's, original or repowered, lasted long enough to make the two- and three-digit renumbering period, nor were any painted orange. Just before those events, the painting diagram was simplified for all black and yellow carbody units - all striping eliminated behind the cab door, etc. Repowered FA 5201 shows off the latest image it will ever wear in Frisco service at St. Louis in October of 1964.

(Louis A. Marre)

Oklahoma City • Quanah

FRISCO

GP-7   GP15-1
GP38AC/-2
GP35   GP40-2

(Left) Frisco's first GP-7 was also EMD's first delivered with the standard Blomberg truck and also the first to have a steam generator for passenger working. This historic unit watches the last light of 1960 fade in the West outside the Tulsa roundhouse. The original painting diagram is still being maintained: full array of yellow nose and frame stripes, thin lettering style on the long hood.
(Collection of E. Gulash)

(Below) Truly "General Purpose," the GP-7's were used for every possible chore on the Frisco during their long tenure. On the Central Division, however, they were the primary road power, because of bridge weight restrictions and tight clearance in the Winslow, AR tunnel. Heavy engineering had to be done to those structures before second-generation power could be used. In the days when the Geeps ruled, daily freight #731 has just crossed the Arkansas River and is in the environs of Ft. Smith on the day after Christmas, 1962, 589 carrying the white flags of an "extra", i.e. second class train.
(Louis A. Marre)

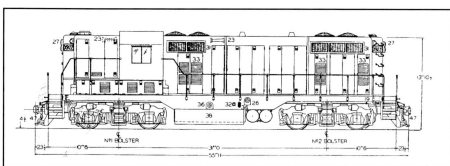

Newburg, MO., 119 miles West of St. Louis, was the crew change point between that city and Springfield. In steam days, it was also a helper station for Dixon Hill, the ruling grade on the main line. By 1955, the helpers were gone, but a local passenger train from St. Louis still made a daily turn to Newburg. Now just Nos. 5 and 6, it was once THE GENERAL WOOD in observance of its real function - a service to Ft. Leonard Wood nearby. A boiler-equipped GP-7, the 612, has brought it West, turned, and will shortly take it back to St. Louis at 12:55 PM. In the interim, an Eastbound Alco-powered freight has arrived and prepares to change crews. Lead FA-1 5216 was later repowered by EMD, in April of 1956.

(M.Morrow/Dischinger Collection)

(Above) In 1961, the painting standard for the GP-7 fleet was simplified for the first time since deliveries had begun in 1950. Nose striping was reduced, and the number of hash marks on the frame halved. Ft. Smith Shops could repaint two units per month, and inherited the task of bringing the forty-odd units assigned to it into conformity. The first two out, 542 and 617, rest amid the wildflowers on July 1, 1961. *(Louis A. Marre)*

(Below) Astrophysicists in search of validation for the hypothesis of a Black Hole - something which swallows light - should give some consideration to a Frisco GP-7 just out of the paint shop. Its reflective yellow striping seems almost to be suspended in mid-air. *(Louis A. Marre)*

(Right) The Extra white flags are firmly in place, venerable caboose 92 is attached, and the Fayetteville Local is ready for work on September 24, 1963, under the capable control of black GP-7 533. *(Mike Condren)*

(Below) Four matched GP-7's in the post-1961 paint scheme appear to be running-board deep in Johnson grass as they pass through the outskirts of Van Buren, AR on August 22, 1963. They are the power of choice for Train #731, shortly to arrive in the terminal at Ft. Smith, just across the Arkansas River. *(Louis A. Marre)*

The Southern half of the Central Division, Ft. Smith, AR to Paris, TX, was generally served on a triweekly basis from Ft. Smith, for it had another outlet - to the "new" Texas main line at Lakeside, OK - which did not have to cross the Kiamichi mountains. Solitary GP-7 541 has this train in hand at Poteau, OK on December 27, 1963 on its southward trip. There are, at this point, only five revenue cars between engine and caboose. *(Louis A. Marre)*

St. Louis-San Francisco Railway Company

and

Quanah, Acme & Pacific Railway Co.

FRISCO

SYSTEM

TIME TABLE NO. 1

Effective
Sunday, October 17, 1971
at 12:01 A. M.
Central Standard Time

SUPERSEDING PREVIOUS TIME TABLES

J. H. BROWN—Vice Pres.-Operation
H. C. BITNER—Gen. Mgr.

FOR EMPLOYES ONLY

The Railway Company reserves the right to vary from the schedules contained herein as circumstances require.

QUANAH, ACME & PACIFIC RAILWAY CO.

1941-1942   Quanah   NO. 266

Pass   Mr. Clarence Waldahl,
             Secretary to Vice-President,
             Fort Worth and Denver City Ry. Co.

RETURNED FOR CANCELLATION
BETWEEN ALL STATIONS
UNTIL DECEMBER 31ST UNLESS OTHERWISE ORDERED
AND SUBJECT TO CONDITIONS ON BACK
VALID WHEN COUNTERSIGNED
BY E. CRABB

E. Crabb   Chas. H. Sommer
                           PRESIDENT

"CHIEF QUANAH"
Last of the Comanches

Frisco acquired control of the minuscule Quanah, Acme & Pacific, a short line from Quanah to Floydada, TX, in hopes of developing a Santa Fe through route via the Floydada connection. That idea was several generations in its payoff, but it was a gold mine when it finally came true. Meanwhile, Frisco dieselized and, in passing, lettered three GP-7's for the QA&P - though it did not, in fact, purchase them on its accounts. QA&P (SL-SF) 546, 547, and 564 were given full Quanah lettering after delivery. The 564 was traded in to EMD in 1964 as QA&P, while the other two were restencilled "Frisco" in 1966. These anomalies are shown here in both guises: QA&P 546 at Ft. Smith on August 8, 1964; Frisco 546 in orange at the same location on May 5, 1966; and boiler-equipped QA&P 564 at Springfield on July 8, 1962.

(Mike Condren)
(Louis A. Marre)
(Louis A. Marre)

Hugo, OK achieved celebrity among gas-electric devotees before WWII by staging a daily three-way meet of cars. By July 2, 1948 when these two photos were made, there were two remaining motorcar schedules meeting in Hugo: #773 and #774 converged there at mid-day from Ardmore, OK and Hope, AR, each continuing to those terminals after the meet. The Hope depot is on the

North-South old main line from Monett to Dallas, so both trains wyed from their East-West route to reach it. EMC car 2121 and its RPO-Baggage trailer are in the foreground, 2124 and its trailer behind. The 2121 was scrapped in 1954, the 2124 sold as a switcher to the Cassville & Exeter in 1952.

(Both photos J.J. Buckley)

(Right) Though the motorcar schedules perished in 1952, rail travelers of 1955 in search of Hope could reach it by a boggling variety of routes ... the one in Arkansas, that is. The St. Louis - Laredo route of the Missouri Pacific's EAGLE fleet offered three trains each way daily which deigned to stop there. The Louisiana & Arkansas portion of the Kansas City Southern terminated the SHREVEPORTER at the MOP connection daily, with a sleeper thence to and from St. Louis and Shreveport. Finally, the Frisco presence at the end of the Lakeside-Hope line of the Central Division was maintained by a train bearing this note in the Official Guide: "Freight Trains 735 and 736 will carry passengers in caboose. Corpses will not be handled." No Hope for the latter? In any case, six and one half hours for the trip of 120 miles allowed plenty of time to long for Hope. Full-striped GP-7 617 approaches Idabel, OK with #736 in June of 1955. *(R.S. Plummer)*

(Below) The boiler-equipped GP-7's were not often called upon for passenger service, as there were plenty of E-7 and E-8s for the main line, and FP-7s for the branches. When the need arose, however, they were available everywhere. On this late October night in 1963, a light snow is falling in Fayetteville, AR while #710 loads mail and express. The 602 is just out of the paint stall at Ft. Smith, and makes a Christmas-card scene. *(Gordon B. Mott)*

(Above) It is June 21, 1964 - the longest day of the year - and First Class Train #710 is an hour gone from Ft. Smith. Time for the evening freight, whose quartet of GP-7's led by 588 rolls past the Yard Office on the way to the North end and twilight departure.

(Mike Condren)

(Below) The mandarin orange and white paint scheme of 1965 was designed with U25B and GP35 power in mind, but it was applied indiscriminately to every other class of power as well. Possibly the first GP-7 to receive the treatment is 571, shown here outside the Car Shop at Springfield on July 10, 1965.

(R.R. Wallin)

(Above) The paint gang has not quite finished with 561 on this November afternoon in 1969. Its fuel tank remains unpainted, but it has been set out to dry along with a lightweight diner lounge from the vanished passenger era now converted to Maintenance of Way equipment. The car's five-digit car number and the green paint where red had been give away its fallen state.

(Mac Owen/Kanak Collection)

(Below) The Frisco line from Monett, MO to Ellsworth, KS via Wichita is subdivided at Neodesha, KS. On June 29, 1971, local freight #5411 is making its smoky way Westward behind a pair of orange GP-7's at Altamont, KS, 31 miles short of its destination. The line from Neodesha to Wichita and Ellsworth is a subdivision of its own, operated in this same style. Lead GP-7 607 still carries its steam generator, if the exhaust stack on the short hood is to be believed, but all passenger trains have been gone for four years, and the boiler is decommissioned if in place. *(Gordon E. Lloyd)*

(Above) While crew members discuss the day's work, GP-7 613 and a GP38-2 await departure from Springfield on a hot June day in 1974. Frisco GP-7's were intended to be secondary-service locomotives, for local freights, way freights, and branch line pas- senger trains. The 613 is one of 52 such units bought with steam heating boilers for passenger service. By this date, the boiler is long since de-activated but the exhaust stack in the short hood indicates that it is still in place. *(Gregory J. Sommers)*

(Left) At least one of the "morphadite" repowered RS-2's received the orange and white livery before they were all retired in 1972. The 553 shows not only that paint in pristine condition, but also a bit of confusion in the paint shop. All Frisco GP units operated short hood forward *except* the RS-2's. Habit overrode observation, and the repaint is stenciled "F" on the front (but wrong) end. Alco RS cab doors were apparently designed for five-foot tall crewmen. That inconvenience plus "back-ward" operation doomed them to booster position 99% of the time - as is here the case, in November of 1970.

(David Cash/ Gordon Lloyd, Jr. Collection)

In the middle of its GP-7 purchasing program, the Frisco paused long enough to sample five competitor RS-2's from Alco. Not a good idea. They were repowered by EMD and became GP-7's in effect, if not appearance, in 1959-60. Two perspectives on the peculiar result are offered here: 551 at Ft. Smith in August, 1961, and 554 riding the turntable there in January, 1963. Long-end front operation remained as Alco had built them. It was just too expensive to turn the controls around as well. *(Louis A. Marre)*

Twenty-five GP15-1's were acquired in 1977 to serve on secondary lines radiating from Hugo, OK. The low maintenance required on these second-generation units brought considerable savings in operating costs on such medium-density trackage. A pair of these, 120 and 113, lead train #738 westbound (timetable North) through Valliant, OK en route to Hugo from the East end of the line, Hope, AR. Valliant was a considerable traffic source: paper from the Weyerhaeuser mill which was itself served by the related Texas, Oklahoma & Eastern short line.

(Gregory J. Sommers)

ANNUAL REPORT 1976
ST. LOUIS-SAN FRANCISCO RAILWAY COMPANY

Two years before merger, Frisco built a new engine service facility at Hugo, OK to take care of the new GP15-1's also bought for this Subdivision. This Sub was a moneymaker because of a Campbell Soup plant in Paris, TX, forest products from the Texas, Oklahoma & Eastern connection at Valliant, OK, Foreman Cement at Foreman, AR, not to mention interchange with KCS at Ashdown, AR and MoPac and KCS at Hope, AR. New GP15-120 is on #738 entering the Hugo yard on April 25, 1978, and five more are seen in the new engine terminal on that same day.

(Gregory J. Sommers)

Five years after the GP38 was introduced in 1966, the Frisco discovered what would become its all-time favorite locomotive. Within the span of five years, 146 examples were purchased, covering two sub-models. The GP38AC's ran from 633 to 662, and the GP38-2's from 663 to 699 and 400 to 478. There were nine separate orders: two for "AC" and seven for "Dash Two" models. The principal differences are illustrated. The 658 is an AC and the 666 a Dash Two, differing only in the bolted-on battery box cover and bolted side window panels on the cab of the Dash Two. The 689 shows the later Dash Two shortened radiator section, and the 476 shows the corrugated radiator found on the last order only. *(Gregory J. Sommers)*

(Above) One of the Frisco's successful pool arrangements was with Seaboard Coast Line. In Birmingham on QLA of May 28, 1972, GP38-2 674 is barely three months old, and a color contrast if nothing more to the mixed bag of SCL GP40's behind: two are still in Seaboard Air Line green and the last one in Atlantic Coast Line black. *(Gordon E. Lloyd)*

(Below) Traffic on the Central Division reached such volume in the last few Frisco years that six units were required for Trains 730/731. Five assorted GP38s and one elderly GP-7 await their #730 call in the humid afternoon of June 27, 1975.

(Louis A. Marre)

(Left) At Staley, OK on April 17, 1978, a Frisco grain train has just entered Missouri - Kansas - Texas Ry. trackage. Within a few feet, it will cross the Red River and enter Texas. The trackage rights are notably short: three tenths of a mile, just enough to cross the river. A pair of GP38's is spliced by a pair of SD45's, with 679 leading. *(Gregory J. Sommers)*

(Below) Four GP38's combine to take a westbound freight through Kirkwood, MO at track speed in August of 1978. Main line trains usually commanded the services of high-horsepower hoods, but the GP38's were all-around utility vehicles, and could handle any assignment if called upon.
(Joe Collias)

Train #731 originated at Springfield and traversed most of the 414 miles to Ft. Smith, AR in the dead of night, arriving at 8 AM. It is being led into Ft. Smith by GP38AC 660 on April 24, 1978. In the second view, the opposite end of the same motive power consist is GP15-1 103, entering the service area. The

power will be serviced and the GP15-1's exchanged for those kept for switching in Ft. Smith or for the tri-weekly train to Hugo, OK. Return Train #731 is scheduled to depart at 10 PM.

(Gregory J. Sommers)

(Above) After leaving the Thayer, MO crew change, Train BTX grinds northward with GP38-2 474 in the lead. The adverse gradient is made more difficult on this February 1979 day by wet and snowy rail.

(Gregory J. Sommers)

(Left) Wreck repairs were contracted out during the 1970's as the Consolidated Mechanical Shops were fully occupied dealing with ever-increasing traffic. GP38-2's 413 and 686 survived a head-on collision at Mustang, OK in September of 1974 and were rebuilt by the Paducah, KY Shops of the Illinois Central Gulf. The rebuilds carried a recognition feature: black numerals on a white background in the number boards. Rebuilt 413 prepares to leave Mobile with an empty export grain train on May 22, 1979.

(Glen P. Koshiol)

(Right) Lilbourn, in the bootheel of Southeast Missouri, witnesses the passage of Train #221 on September 18, 1979. The lead unit, GP38AC 652, is one of thirty purchased in early 1971. Frisco ownership of GP38's reached a total of 146 at the end of 1976.
(Gregory J. Sommers)

(Below) In September 1979, there were but two daily trains in each direction on the scenic River Division, which extended from the end of Lindenwood Yard in St. Louis to Turrell, AR, where it joined the Kansas City to Memphis main line. The daylight southbound, Train #221, is just in the process of changing crews at Chaffee, MO on Sept. 23rd. *(Gregory J. Sommers)*

(Above) On the last morning of 1979, Train #730 rumbles majestically over the composite Frog River bridge at Mountainburg, AR. Normally a night train, its daylight passage through the Boston Mountains is due to the New Year holiday schedule, advanced by twelve hours so as to get the crew home to Springfield before midnight. The blue and white Rock Island boxcars in the train are to lose their corporate owner three months hence. The locomotives will lose theirs in November of the new year. *(Gregory J. Sommers)*

(Below) New Year's Day of 1980 finds one of the Cherokee Yard GP38AC's, the 656, looking into the future. By the end of this new year, the Frisco will have ceased to exist, and shortly after that this unit will turn into a green Burlington Northern #2132. *(Gregory J. Sommers)*

ST. LOUIS-SAN FRANCISCO
RAILWAY COMPANY

FRISCO

SPECIAL INSTRUCTIONS
FOR

**TIME TABLE
No. 3**

MEMPHIS TERMINAL
DIVISION

Effective Wednesday, January 1, 1975
at 12:01 A.M. Central Standard Time

Superseding Previous Time Tables

H. C. Bitner - Gen. Mgr.
V. J. Deckard - Senior Ass't. Gen. Mgr.
B. C. Davidson - Ass't. Gen. Mgr.

FOR EMPLOYES ONLY

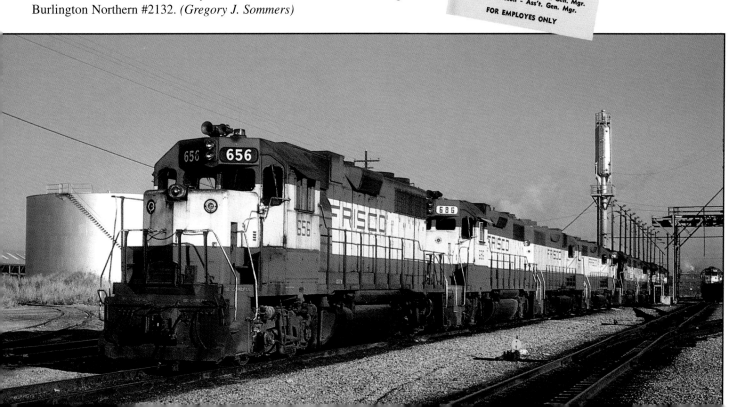

(Above) Columbus, KS is the junction of Frisco's line from Edward (Ft. Scott) KS to Afton, OK with the line from Pierce City, MO to Wichita, KS. Train #139 is working through Columbus on May 11, 1980 with GP38-2 429 in the lead, headed for Tulsa. *(Gregory J. Sommers)*

(Left) Daily-except-Sunday local #2011, with GP38-2 452 and GP35 710 for power, heads South through Pevely, MO on May 8, 1980. The River Division local (and its counterpart #2010) made the 136.5 mile trek between Lindenwood and Chaffee in just under six hours, doing what local work there was en route. *(Gregory J. Sommers)*

91

The Frisco was an early believer in pooled power arrangements which let locomotives as well as their trains pass from one member road to another. A pool with Missouri Pacific was unusual, however, in that it was with a competitor more than a connection. The arrangement developed to serve a Union Electric coal-fired power plant on the River Division, and Frisco's contribution was a set of eight GP38-2's with heavy-duty six-cylinder air compressors and extra trainline connections for air-dump hoppers. But, as usual, special units tend to

stray away, and anything else will have to do. These two photos illustrate the phenomenon. In the upper view, customized 426-433 are nowhere to be found, and plain vanilla 637 and 642 are teamed with MoPac U23B 2260 on the train in the MP's Dolton, IL yard on September 12, 1977. The action view is of the train heading South on Frisco itself, at Afton, MO in September, 1978 - again with an ordinary GP38-2 in charge, in this instance the 409, and an assisting pair of blue MP U23B's.

(Glen Koshiol) (Joe Collias)

(Right) Afton, MO is a railroad location 11.6 miles South of Southeast Junction, the St. Louis starting point of the River Division. Though crooked, the Division is a low-grade line, and GP38's were the usual power for the two through trains each way and the tri-weekly locals. The Union Electric coal trains were also in charge of GP38's as the Frisco contribution to the Missouri Pacific pool agreement which brought them to St. Louis to be forwarded. A pair of clean GP38-2's led by 437 is charging past Afton in September of 1978 with the local, Train #2011. *(Joe Collias)*

(Below) Frisco skipped the GP20 and GP30 generation of EMD road power, though it received proposals for them and hosted demonstrations in the normal course of business. The general success of the pioneering GE U25Bs notwithstanding, EMD was returned to in 1964 for their 2500 h.p. competitor, the GP35. Having 3000 gallons of fuel on board was essential if an operating range equivalent to the U25's was to be obtained, so for the first order an extra-capacity fuel tank was specified. To make room for it, the air reservoirs were moved from under the frame to the top of the hood, and a "torpedo boat" look arrived on the road. The last unit of that first order, 716 heads a pair of U25Bs and another GP35 in Kansas City's 19th. Street service track on August 4, 1964 -- four months old. *(Louis A. Marre)*

(Above) First-order "torpedo boat" GP35s were the last locomotives to be delivered in the black and yellow paint scheme. Mandarin orange and white, inspired by a demonstration tour of the GP35 and DD35 which were painted by EMD in a similar design, was the standard from February 14, 1965. The first new units in the orange scheme were eight U25B's delivered in March, 1965 - 816-823. The 823, just a month old, makes a vivid punctuation mark amid three black GP35's, led by 706, leaving St. Louis on May 1, 1965. *(Mike Condren)*

(Above) By October 26, 1968, when black GP35 706 waited its turn for service at Springfield, orange and white was the standard paint scheme, as seen on U25B 803 just behind. That portion of 706's fuel tank above the horizontal seam is the extra section welded on to a regulation EMD tank for additional fuel capacity, which in turn displaces the air reservoirs to their unusual rooftop location. *(Elliott Kahn)*

Crystal City, MO is located at mile 40.0 on the River Division. From that point to Cape Girardeau, at mile 131.6, the line closely follows the Mississippi River, thus making it vulnerable to closure during periods of high water. All is dry on June 17, 1974 however, when GP35 703 leads U25B's 819 and 820 on the point of Train #833 through Crystal City. *(Gregory J. Sommers)*

(Above) Down the River Division some 28 miles below Southeast Junction in St. Louis, GP35 706 is bracketed by a pair of semaphores as it makes its way South with Train #221 on December 7, 1974.

(Joe Collias)

FRISCO

5,000 MILES Serving:

Missouri
Kansas
Arkansas
Oklahoma
Texas
Tennessee
Mississippi
Alabama
Florida

(Below) In this view from the hump tower at Cherokee Yard in June of 1975, we see GP35 719 and three GP38-2's headed West. The 719 was one of the first units delivered in the mandarin orange and white paint scheme, adopted in 1965. Its inspiration came from a demonstration tour of the EMD GP35/DD35 set which was painted in a similar fashion. No DD35's came to the Frisco, but the GP35 and the second generation paint came and stayed to the end of Frisco independence. (Gregory J. Sommers)

(Above) Returning from a heavy UP transfer delivery, GP35 707, two GP38's and a caboose are on their way back to Rosedale Yard in Kansas City, KS on September 2, 1978. It was not uncommon to find Union Pacific units on the Frisco, as the two roads did a heavy interchange traffic.

(Bob Graham)

(Below) Toward the end of Frisco independence, it was common to find GP35 or SD45 units in storage during slack periods. Both models were, by the standards of the GP40/GP38 era, less fuel-efficient. Awaiting a return to duty there are four GP35s in temporary storage at Tulsa on January 1, 1980. *(Gregory J. Sommers)*

ST. LOUIS-SAN FRANCISCO
••• RAILWAY •••

Ship it on
the Frisco

SOUTHEAST·SOUTHWEST

SOUTH EAST
WEST

(Above) What we think of as the "Main Line" of the Frisco to Dallas/Ft. Worth is, in fact, the second such line. The original route from the 1880's was the Central Division, via Ft. Smith, AR to Paris, TX and thence to Dallas over the Santa Fe on trackage rights. Northbound on this "new" main line is an extra freight headed by GP35 726, passing rapidly through Scullin, OK on May 13, 1980. This order of GP35's (725-731) rides on trade-in Alco trucks and, because of their longer wheelbase, has 2850 gallon fuel tanks rather than the usual 3000 gal.

(Gregory J. Sommers)

(Above) During the final three years of independence, the Frisco remained committed to service improvements. Five new locomotive models were added to the roster, and a sixth (the GP50) was ordered but delivered after the Burlington Northern merger had taken effect. The two largest new groups were the 25 GP15-1's and 25 GP40-2's. Two-week-old GP40-2 (and the "class unit") 750 is spending a few minutes in Tennessee Yard on May 18, 1979. *(Gregory J. Sommers)*

(Above) Maximum mainline speed for most trains was 55 MPH, but hottest of hot Trains 32, 33, and QLA were permitted 60. Train 33 is making the allowed mile a minute through Brookline, MO on May 17, 1980 with the newest power, led by GP40-2 772. Trains 32 and 33 were marketed as the TEXAS SPECIAL, a name fragrant with the memory of the joint Frisco-MKT passenger train discontinued in 1959. *(Gregory J. Sommers)*

(Below) Only four or five months old, four gleaming GP40-2's make a flying crew change at the yard office in Springfield before continuing East with Train #32. The new crew is on, the gyralite is flashing, and 12,000 shiny EMD horses are beginning to dig in. It is, however, October 13, 1979: Frisco has only a bit more than a year to live free. *(J. Harlen Wilson)*

(Above) On a fine September afternoon in 1979, a matched quartet of new GP40-2's rattles the Missouri Pacific's Carondelet Sub diamond in Kirkwood, MO, leaving St. Louis with the TEXAS SPECIAL Train 33. So well were the GP40-2's suited to Frisco's hottest trains that considerable regret was expressed by management that they had not obtained some much earlier. (Joe Collias)

(Below) Howling at full track speed of 60 m.p.h., three new GP40-2's roll Train #38 over new welded rail through Ravia, OK on May 13, 1980. The GP40-2's turned out to be ideal for such hot trains as this, and spent their entire short Frisco lives in such service. (Gregory J. Sommers)

(Right) The last new locomotive delivered to the St. Louis - San Francisco Ry. is GP40-2 774. It waits for a crew outside the Lindenwood Diesel Shop on May 8, 1980. Four GP40-2's were the customary power for Train #33 from delivery until the BN merger. The 774 went into service on June 21, 1979, and so the reign of the GP40's on #33 lasted almost exactly eighteen months.
(Gregory J. Sommers)

(Below) The last new locomotive delivered to the St. Louis - San Francisco Railway Company shakes Kirkwood with turbocharged fury in June, 1980, at the head of four GP40-2's on Train #33. The full light array includes a Gyralite and white classification lights. *(Joe Collias)*

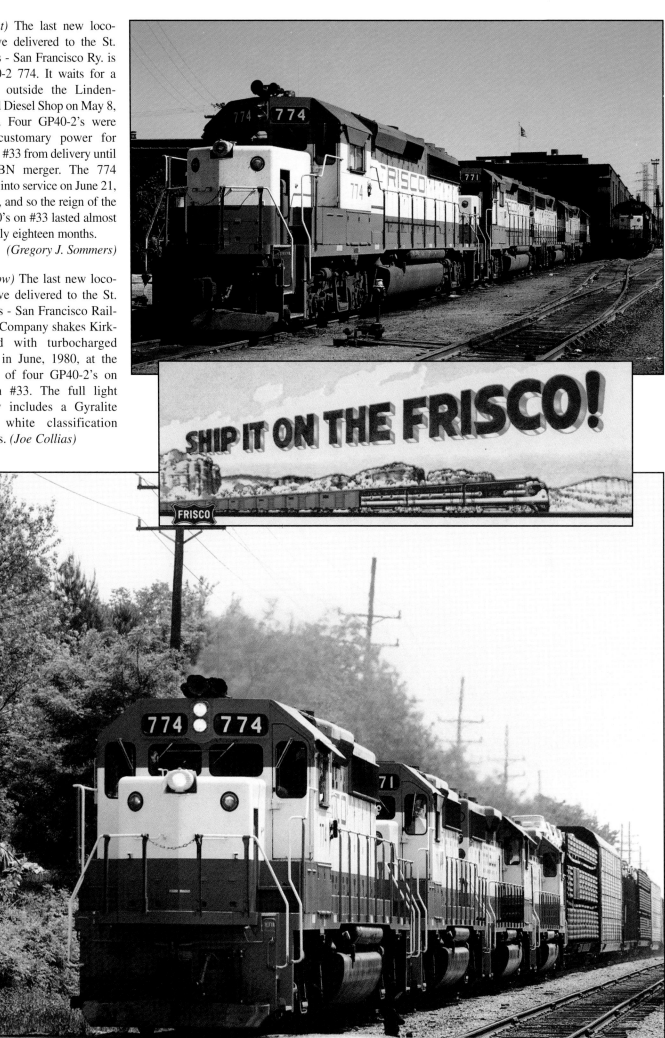

FRISCO

U25B
U30B
B30-7

Before purchasing the very first U25B's, Frisco hosted and tested the experimental prototype, GE 751. It is shown here at Springfield in multiple with an FP-7 (only one demo unit was tested) on November 3, 1960. The first production units came with high short hoods like the 751, but there were significant differences in the design. The 751 was never sold, but returned eventually to Erie to languish for decades as a hollow carcass behind the Works. *(R.R. Wallin)*

(Above) The first four GE high-horsepower, four-axle domestic locomotives built for a customer are Frisco 800-803 of December, 1961. This view of the 803 on the service tracks outside the Springfield Diesel Shop on July 8, 1962 shows the high short hood and earliest carbody details of the very first U-Boats to go into regular service on a U.S. carrier. (*Louis A. Marre*)

(Below) Three "torpedo boats" and one U-Boat approach the tower guarding the multiple crossings of the Texas & Pacific, the MKT, and the Santa Fe in Tulsa on June 6, 1964. All-black second generation hoods rule the main this year. The 810 is one of a four-unit second U25B order delivered just one year earlier, and the fourteen units of the first GP35 order are barely two months old at this time. (*Emery Gulash*)

(Above) This right side view of U25B 803 shows a GP35 as the second unit. All are still in black, though the photo dates from September 23, 1967 - nearly six years after the first U25's arrived. The freight-unit-paint car in the right background is a steam generator car, a former baggage car converted to a steam heat supply for troop trains and special moves that might have to use freight locomotives. Passenger service on the entire railroad ceased just fourteen months after this photo. *(Louis A. Marre)*

(Below) By 1960, Frisco had settled on the EMD F or GP unit for all road freight. What a shock, then, was the purchase of the absolutely new General Electric U25B in 1961. Only Frisco and the Union Pacific purchased the high-nose version. Here is freshly repainted 805 in the sun at Lindenwood in June of 1973, twelve years after the revolution. *(Gregory J. Sommers)*

(Above) Differences between the first and last carbody designs of General Electric's U25B's are evident in this view outside the system Diesel Shop in Springfield, MO on November 25, 1973. The 801 was Frisco's second U25 and 830 its second from last. The first eight were high-nose versions, the rest low-nose. All of the first eight were traded back to GE for B30-7's 863-870 in 1977. GE in turn leased them to Conrail briefly, but then all were scrapped. *(Gregory J. Sommers)*

(Below) Frisco used Southern Pacific trackage rights to traverse the Sherman/Denison TX area for about ten miles. Train #531, led by U25B 828, approaches its terminal there with connection traffic for its landlord on April 27, 1978. *(Gregory J. Sommers)*

(Above) Three U25B's (805-800-823) await a clearance in Lindenwood Yard for Train #833, a River Division train to Memphis. By this May 1974 date, fully matched U25 consists led by the high-nosed originals were increasingly rare. The high-noses were all off the roster by September 1977. (Gregory J. Sommers)

(Below) The last example of the U25B model built by General Electric happened to be for the Frisco, which also had purchased the very first. The 831 is shown here leading a train into Tennessee Yard with two high and wide special loads from Birmingham in September of 1979. (Gregory J. Sommers)

(Left) With a total of only 71 units by General Electric, Frisco managed within that limit to have the first and last U25B, the first U30B and the first B30-7. For good measure, 846 is the first "XR" series unit, i.e. a sub-model of the U30B with some reliability enhancements and GE's 2500th U-series locomotive. Suitably monogrammed 846 is shown here at Springfield in October of 1975. *(Collection of Glen P. Koshiol)*

(Below) Extra 845 South, led by the U30B of that number, leaves Springfield for Memphis on January 2, 1980. An SD40-2 and SD45 are the second and third units respectively. *(Gregory J. Sommers)*

The U30B's lacked the novelty of the U25 fleet and the second-generation hi-tech look of the B30's, and so remained somewhat inconspicuous in Frisco operations. The 857 is a businesslike hood nonetheless, seen in St. Louis in August 1975.
(Gregory J. Sommers)

FRISCO

annual report
1 9 6 9

St. Louis – San Francisco Railway Company

(Above) Hotshot CTB sails above the Coldwater River just south of Olive Branch, MS on May 18, 1979, led by freshly-repainted U30B 833, with similarly spiffy 834 as third unit. The modern concrete bridge is one example of Frisco's determined upgrading of its physical plant to the very end of its independence.

(Gregory J. Sommers)

(Below) The final GE order by the Frisco was for eight B30-7's, 863-870, delivered at the very end of 1977. They had, therefore, just three years to run before the merger at the end of 1980 converted their mandarin orange to Cascade green. The 868 is leading the charge of Train #33 across the MoPac's Carondelet Subdivision in Kirkwood, MO on a fine April afternoon in 1980. *(Joe Collias)*

(Above) Train #33 provided next-morning Dallas-Fort Worth service from St. Louis and was, therefore, a very hot train indeed. It is shown here rolling expeditiously through Crescent, MO on August 8, 1979 behind B30-7 866 and two SD40-2's.

(Gregory J. Sommers)

(Below) There were only eight B30-7's on the Frisco roster, and they were not restricted to any specific train or service. The odds against finding half of them on one train were, therefore, extremely remote. Nevertheless, four of the eight are in full throttle with TEXAS SPECIAL #33 near Lebanon, MO on May 14, 1979. Units traded back to GE for these B30's included the very first Frisco (and consequently the builder's first) U25B's.

(Gregory J. Sommers)

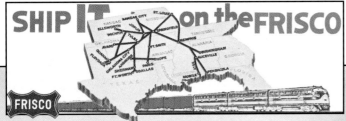

FRISCO

SD38-2
SD40-2
SD45

(Above) Even a pair of SW1500's were inadequate when it came to working the hump pusher jobs in Tulsa and Memphis. Four SD38-2's were purchased in 1979 specifically for these assignments. Tulsa's Cherokee Yard hump is a "hold back" rather than "push" operation, so 296 and 297 came with extended range dynamic braking for this unusual operation. The 297 is shown in tandem with SW1500 358 on New Year's Day of 1980. The "switcher numbers" assigned to these units clearly indicated their intended use. *(Gregory J. Sommers)*

(Below) For the Tennessee Yard hump, Frisco bought two SD38-2's without the dynamic brakes specified for the Cherokee Yard's downhill hump. Special features for the both pairs included heavy duty braking (two brake cylinders for each axle), high-strength draft gear and couplers, and hump control. The 299 is caught between shoves on April 1, 1980. *(J. Harlen Wilson)*

(Above) Eight SD40-2's arrived on the Frisco in July, 1978, fully eight years after the last SD45. They were intended for an Oklahoma unit coal train which never materialized and so they spent their two years on the road in general freight service. They were more at home after the Burlington Northern merger, where they had eight hundred others for company. On the Frisco, they were rare birds and hard to catch. One, the 955, is seen here on Train 131 at Marshfield, MO, May 10, 1980.

(Gregory J. Sommers)

(Below) Since the eight SD40-2's were only on the road some eighteen months before merger day, they were elusive because of their small number. They were neither in nor out of favor - just spread thin. When the Fates smiled, any of them could turn in a creditable job. Consider, for example, the 951 rattling the MoPac diamond in Kirkwood with hotshot #33 on Labor Day of 1979.

(Joe Collias)

By the time of this photograph on May 10, 1980, the Burlington Northern + Frisco merger had received Interstate Commerce Commission approval, and awaited only the disposition of several appeals by competitors to be effected. In this twilight period, business proceeded as usual. Train #131 hustles through Willow Springs, MO behind SD40-2 955, an SD45 and a GP38-2. *(Gregory J. Sommers)*

(Above) On Frisco main lines, the "Cadillacs" of the roster were the forty-nine SD45's. They were the highest horsepower units on the road from delivery to merger, and were assigned to the hottest of trains up to the very end. In May of 1979, two of them and an aged U25B are accelerating a train out of the crew change at Amory, MS towards Birmingham, AL. *(Gregory J. Sommers)*

(Below) The Union electric coal train operated jointly with Missouri Pacific grinds through Afton, MO in August of 1978 with more than the usual four GP38 or U23B power: Frisco SD45 925, two Union Pacific U30C's and two Frisco GP38's for a total of 13,600 horses. *(Joe Collias)*

(Right) Of all Frisco orange and white road-switchers, only four carried nose-mounted heralds: SD45's 911, 912 and 915 plus GP38AC 651. These were applied during repaintings or repairs, but never spread to the entire roster. The 911 is shown here next to un-heralded GP40-2 773 by way of comparison.

(Gregory J. Sommers)

(Below) At Mile 196 of the River Division, between Conran and Portageville, MO on May 25, 1979, daytime through freight #221 rolls into view under leadership of SD45 922. The "L" shaped engineer's window is conspicuous, but increasingly expensive to maintain at this point. From 1979 to the end of independence, there was a program afoot to replace them with conventional glass. Frisco maintained its property to the very end.

(Gregory J. Sommers)

196.0

(Left) Frisco concern over rail wear caused by six-axle units is not reflected in the immaculate condition of freshly-painted SD45 912 in the 19th Street Yard in Kansas City, MO on September 8, 1979. There was, however, an eight-year hiatus in six-axle power purchasing after the last SD45. Only when new coal business seemed assured were eight SD40-2's ordered, and when that business evaporated, four-axle hoods were the standard again. *(Gregory J. Sommers)*

(Below) Dynamic brakes howling at maximum amperage, two SD45's and a GP40-2 approach the crew change point of Thayer, MO in May of 1979. They are on the OBX train, originating in Tulsa and destined for Birmingham. Gyralite warning lights on the noses of the final order of SD45's, 943-948, are the result of a decision to equip new power from 1969 onwards with that safety device.

(Gregory J. Sommers)

(Above) First light in Mem-phis discloses SD45 947 and company arriving at Tenn-essee Yard with the CTB train from Tulsa - **C**herokee, **T**ennessee, **B**irmingham supplying the yard initials for the symbol. This is a hot train, carrying Santa Fe traffic to the Seaboard Coast Line at Birmingham. On this Sep-tember 28, 1979, the two SD45's are assisted by no fewer than four GP38-2's

(Gregory J. Sommers)

(Left) On a snowy February day in 1979, a pair of SD45's and a single GP35 work together to grind a heavy drag past Koshkonong, MO, nine miles north of the crew change at Thayer. The stretch of line from Thayer all the way to Norwood has the steepest grades on the entire Kansas City to Memphis main. At this point, an SD45 was rated for only 2100 tons, a GP35 at 1615 tons - the lowest tonnage ratings on any Frisco main line.

(Gregory J. Sommers)

(Above) It was common to add one four-motor unit to a pair of six-axle SD40 or SD45 units to maintain optimum tractive effort at the higher end of the speed/tractive effort curve. A demonstration of this power combination is provided here by SD45's 934 and 929 assisted by U25B 808 on the CTB train at Willow Springs, MO on May 10, 1979. *(Gregory J. Sommers)*

(Below) The "Cadillac" SD45's remained in top-line service to the very end of Frisco independence. Two of them have undertaken to forward the TEXAS SPECIAL train, #33, from Lindenwood to Springfield on February 14, 1980. Leading 933 has retained its L-shaped engineer's window. *(Joe Collias)*

FRISCO

Business Cars
Passenger Cars
Cabooses
Freight Cars
Wrecking Cranes

(Above) The premier business car in the Fifties was the *Saint Louis* and the second was, fittingly enough, the *San Francisco*. Business of very high level has brought a gilded cage to Ft. Smith, and it is shown here wearing the markers on Train 710 just prior to its 6:15 PM departure - which you can bet will be on time today - on August 15, 1961. Shortly after this date, the business car fleet was reduced sharply (to two cars from seven) and numbered, rather than named. *(Louis A. Marre)*

(Below) By the time this photo was taken in March, 1974, the business car "fleet" had been reduced to only two cars, Nos. 1 and 2, formerly *Missouri* and *Saint Louis* respectively. The cars were maintained in the remnant of the passenger car shop in Springfield, where No. 2 is seen. *(Gregory J. Sommers)*

When orange and white paint had been the locomotive standard for ten years, someone decided that the Pullman green business cars needed the same treatment. In a gaudy new dress, Car 1 makes a debut in Springfield in August, 1975. Somehow the effect is not entirely what was desired. Built by American Car & Foundry in 1912 as a coach, the car was first converted into a diner, then a business car, all by Springfield Shop. In 1912, such colors were unthinkable, and they are not a particularly good idea six decades later. *(Gregory J. Sommers)*

Heavyweight cafe-lounge *Birmingham* was among several older cars cosmetically treated to match the postwar lightweight equipment for the METEOR and TEXAS SPECIAL, which never had quite enough new cars to go around. With red paint and some stainless steel siding, it stands in the consist of the KANSAS CITY - FLORIDA SPECIAL, with the American Royal buildings in the background, at Kansas City on July 16, 1955. The improvements do not entirely conceal a 96-ton behemoth of WW I vintage.
(E. Gulash Collection)

With the exceptions of some First Class amenity cars such as the lounge *Birmingham* above and some Pullman sleepers, the Frisco's older passenger equipment remained in conservative Pullman green with yellow lettering. Heavyweight coach *Okmulgee* at Tulsa in June, 1964 is a fair representative.
(Collias Collection)

One of the Pullman-Standard lightweight baggage-RPO cars from the streamlining of the METEOR has just been overhauled and repainted at Springfield Shops in January of 1960, and is literally drying its paint in the sun at the depot before returning to service. *(Collias Collection)*

Among other noteworthy achievements, the Frisco pioneered the use of multilevel rack cars for the transport of new automobiles. The very earliest cars were built from the rail up, much different from subsequent practice which put a rack atop a conventional TTX flatcar. One of these early cars, SLSF 3356, is seen here on the New York Central at Toledo, Ohio in August, 1963, loaded with a local product - Jeeps from the Toledo Assembly. The car itself is only six months old. *(Emery Gulash)*

Along with the rest of the industry, Frisco soon began to mount company-owned auto racks atop TTX-owned flats. RTTX 910887 is three layers deep in Chryslers on the Wabash at Melvindale, MI in November of 1964. The next stage in auto rack evolution covered the load to protect against vandalism en route.

(Emery Gulash)

(Above and right) Frisco employed a color code on boxcars which were restricted to specific customers. Car 15041 was rebuilt in 1967 by Chicago Freight Car for cereal loading, and adorned in a version of locomotive mandarin orange. The 700296 was built new by Pacific Car & Foundry in 1977 and assigned to beer loading for the Schlitz brewery in Memphis. Its beige color was apparently an attempt to simulate the color of the car's usual lading Frisco. *(Gregory J. Sommers)*

On the Frisco, a boxcar painted yellow had a cushioned underframe; beige was for beer; and blue, orange, gray, and boxcar red also had occult significance. Shiny cushioned car 6127 awaits movement from Springfield in February, 1974.

(Gregory J. Sommers)

"*Ship it on the Frisco!*" That slogan adorned most boxcars, reefers, cabooses, and even some covered hoppers. Over the years, some style changes were made: the "*Southeast ... Southwest*" addition was dropped after 1970; black backgrounds were not renewed after 1977. Some of these changes are represented here. PS-1 boxcar 21024 was repainted and is in Springfield in January 1974, while 22015 was repainted in August 1978, and is seen in Thayer, MO in June 1979. *(Gregory J. Sommers)*

In southern Oklahoma and in parts of Alabama and Mississippi, considerable forest product traffic moved over the Frisco. One of a modest fleet of special cars for that traffic is woodchip hopper

93108, shown here after a recent overhaul in 1979.

(Gregory J. Sommers)

Frisco ordered three hundred covered hoppers from Pullman-Standard in 1980. It was decided to have these painted in Burlington Northern's Cascade Green rather than Frisco's standard gray. The rationale was that after merger the BN lettering could be easily applied. The BN proved incapable of such subtlety, and the entire class had to await full repainting before relettering. Car 86583, at Winchester, KY in October of 1991 (ten years after merger) illustrates one of the escapees. *(Gregory J. Sommers)*

A late survivor of vanished passenger operation is Frisco express boxcar 467, seen in use as a storage barn at Kansas City, MO on May 3, 1970. Its Pullman green paint and gold lettering mark it as a former component of first-class trains. *(Owen Leander)*

Some of the Pullman lightweight passenger equipment bought for the METEOR and TEXAS SPECIAL in 1948 was adapted for non-revenue service after the end of all passenger operation. MW 11251, shorn of its stainless steel trim and red paint, is a sad remnant of former glory at Amory, MS on February 9, 1979. It is hard to imagine that it was once deluxe 56-seat coach *Pasadena Hills* and regularly ran behind matched and named E-8's.

(Gregory J. Sommers)

The heaviest wrecking cranes on the Frisco (and the first diesels) were 250-ton capacity Industrial Brownhoists, two of which are shown here at work. Springfield's 99022 is shown almost new and in original black paint working on a derailment near home c. 1955. The silver paint which became the standard about 1960 is shown on 99025, cleaning up a yard mishap at Memphis on October 30, 1977. Like most others, Frisco sold off most of its wrecking equipment in the Seventies in favor of contracting out and of highway vehicles.
(M. Morrow/Dischinger Collection)
(Gregory J. Sommers)

Construction of cabooses from salvaged PS-1 boxcars was in full swing at the Consolidated Mechanical Shop in the summer of 1974. These two views show a boxcar in the throes of conversion as well as a line of pre-fabricated cupolas ready for installation.
(Gregory J. Sommers)

Venerable outside-braced wooden caboose 157 is obviously in superb mechanical condition despite its apparent age in Tulsa, June, 1964. *(E. Gulash)*

(Right) The first all-steel waycars on the Frisco were seventy-five "Wide-Vision" models built by International Car at Kenton, Ohio in 1957. The "Wide-Vision" denotes the cupolas which extend beyond the side wall dimension of the carbody as well as above the roofline. Originally numbered 200-274, they were renumbered in 1968 to 1200-1274, thus avoiding computer data conflict with the 200-series diesel switchers. At Amory, MS on May 23, 1979, the 1216 awaits its next run.*(Gregory J. Sommers)*

(Below) A nearly-new Wide-Vision caboose shows clearly the as-built appearance of the group at Ft. Scott, KS in August, 1958. *(E. Gulash)*

Early in 1978, cabooses began to share the orange and white paint scheme applied to locomotives since 1965. A freshly painted 1260 illustrates the new image at Lindenwood on February 4, 1979. The General Steel caboose truck is apparent in this view - the best-riding design on the railroad, according to an unscientific poll of conductors. *(Gregory J. Sommers)*

(Left) By 1970 it was evident that replacements for remaining wooden cabooses were needed, especially to fill the demands for run-through trains with Union Pacific and Seaboard Coast Line. The Consolidated Mechanical Shops (aka Springfield Shops) designed a waycar that could be built economically by adaptation of Pullman-Standard PS-1 forty-foot boxcars, very much surplus by 1970 standards. The "class unit" 1700 is shown at Tennessee Yard on September 28, 1979. Its humble origins are apparent. *(Gregory J. Sommers)*

Frisco's last cabooses were built at the Consolidated Mechanical Shops in Springfield, using PS-1 boxcars as it had done since 1971. The final ten, 1725-1735, came out in 1979 at the very end of independence. The change to a bay-window from a cupola style was brought about in part by increasing freight car height - especially auto racks - which made cupola visibility useless. The first bay window built by CMS awaits departure from Cherokee Yard on May 13, 1980.

(Gregory J. Sommers)

By 1974, most railroads had painted various pieces of equipment in some patriotic design to observe the approaching Bicentennial. Although proposals were made to paint an SD45 in a red/white/blue scheme, the Frisco confined its observance to three cabooses. The 1776, shown here in St. Louis in June of

1974, and 1250 in Memphis in November of 1977, demonstrate the two painting diagrams used. The other example was 1237, which matched the 1250. By 1980, all had been repainted into standard orange and white. *(Gregory J. Sommers)*